# STOCKHOLM
## ENCOUNTER

**BECKY OHLSEN**

Stockholm Encounter

**Published by Lonely Planet Publications Pty Ltd**
ABN 36 005 607 983

| | |
|---|---|
| **Australia** | Head Office, Locked Bag 1, Footscray, Vic 3011 |
| | ☎ 03 8379 8000 fax 03 8379 8111 |
| | talk2us@lonelyplanet.com.au |
| **USA** | 150 Linden St, Oakland, CA 94607 |
| | ☎ 510 893 8555 |
| | toll free 800 275 8555 |
| | fax 510 893 8572 |
| | info@lonelyplanet.com |
| **UK** | 2nd fl, 186 City Rd, London EC1V 2NT |
| | ☎ 020 7106 2100 fax 020 7106 2101 |
| | go@lonelyplanet.co.uk |

This title was commissioned in Lonely Planet's London office and produced by: **Commissioning Editor** Jo Potts **Coordinating Editor** Barbara Delissen **Coordinating Cartographer** Corey Hutchison **Layout Designer** Jim Hsu **Assisting Editor** Michala Green **Assisting Cartographer** Khanh Luu **Managing Editor** Imogen Bannister **Managing Cartographer** David Connolly **Cover** Image research provided by lonelyplanetimages.com **Project Manager** Sarah Sloane **Thanks to** Jessica Boland, Sally Darmody, Laura Jane, Wayne Murphy, Cara Smith, Herman So, Lyahna Spencer

ISBN 978 1 74179 286 7

Printed through Colorcraft Ltd, Hong Kong.
Printed in China

# HOW TO USE THIS BOOK
## Colour-Coding & Maps

Colour-coding is used for symbols on maps and in the text that they relate to (eg all eating venues on the maps and in the text are given a green knife and fork symbol). Each neighbourhood also gets its own colour, and this is used down the edge of the page and throughout that neighbourhood section.

Shaded yellow areas on the maps denote 'areas of interest' – for their historical significance, their attractive architecture or their great bars and restaurants. We encourage you to head to these areas and just start exploring!

**Send us your feedback** We love to hear from readers – your comments help make our books better. We read every word you send us, and we always guarantee that your feedback goes straight to the appropriate authors. The most useful submissions are rewarded with a free book. To send us your updates and find out about Lonely Planet events, newsletters and travel news visit our award-winning website: *lonelyplanet .com/contact*.

Note: We may edit, reproduce and incorporate your comments in Lonely Planet products such as guidebooks, websites and digital products, so let us know if you don't want your comments reproduced or your name acknowledged. For a copy of our privacy policy visit *lonelyplanet.com/privacy*.

**Mixed Sources**
Product group from well-managed forests and other controlled sources
www.fsc.org Cert no. SGS-COC-005002
© 1996 Forest Stewardship Council

## BECKY OHLSEN

Becky has written about Sweden for Lonely Planet several times; she visits Stockholm at least twice a year to spend time with friends and relatives and to get a sneak-peek at the fashion trends that will eventually reach her home town of Portland, Oregon, many months later. She loves Stockholm's saffron-coloured buildings and fantastic museums and is particularly fond of the view from the Söder hills.

### BECKY'S THANKS

Thanks go to Cristian Bonetto for a stellar 1st edition of this book, and to Jo Potts for assigning me the job of updating it. I'm also very grateful to my interview subjects: Jennifer Spratly, Daniel Lampinen, Sara Arrhenius at Bonniers Konsthall, Erika and Ulrika Larsson at Normal, Lina the bartender, and Lydia Kellam of the Swede Beat.

## THE PHOTOGRAPHER

Raised in the Scottish Highlands, Jonathan Smith graduated from St Andrews University in 1994 with an MA in German. Unsure of what to do with his life, he took a flight to Vilnius and spent the next four years travelling around the former USSR. Having tried everything from language teaching to translating Lithuanian cookery books into English, Jon resolved to seek his fortune as a freelance travel photographer. Since then Jon's byline has appeared in over 50 Lonely Planet titles.

**Our Readers** Many thanks to the travellers who wrote to us with helpful hints, useful advice and interesting anecdotes. Guy Badman, Fredrik Blomberg, Kristin Bray, Lauren Geilhufe, Alexander Gotthard Real, Gwenno Jones, Blair Rodger, Valerie Schnee, Isabell Skarby Hay, Esther Span-Murre, Mario Toups, Anne Wouters

**Cover photograph** Art in a Tunnelbana station, Siegfried Stolzfuss/eStock Photo
**Internal photographs** p46 by Sara Arrhenius; pp144-5 by Anders Blomqvist; pp10-11 by dayhot image/Leif Davidsson/Alamy; p18 by Greg Elms; p16 by Christer Fredriksson; p96 by Dorothea Kaufmann; p130 Lydia Kellam; p6, p50 by Martin Llado; p6 by Ernest Manewal; p23 by www.mrrichardryan.com; p6, p20, p24, pp32-3, p43, p60, p158, p159 by Jonathan Smith; p137 by Wayne Walton. All other photographs by Lonely Planet Images and by Jonathan Smith.

All images are copyright of the photographers unless otherwise indicated. Many of the images in this guide are available for licensing from **Lonely Planet Images:** lonelyplanetimages.com.

The trendy streets of SoFo (p94)

# CONTENTS

# THIS IS STOCKHOLM

Straddling 14 islands where the Baltic meets Lake Mälaren, this shiny Nordic star seems to have it all – edgy creativity, inner-city forests and waterways clean enough for a bracing downtown dip.

Here, heritage and hip live side by side; urbanites toast the spring with old-school tunes and wooden huts sidle up to modernist blocks. Washing the lot is a pure northern light, from ice-blue winter tones to amber autumn hues. It hits the earthy red and saffron buildings and makes them glow with fairy-tale appeal.

The city's eye-candy factor extends to its well-travelled denizens, often gorgeous and enviably fashion-literate . After all, this is home turf to street-smart labels like Acne, Nudie and Patrik Söderstam, all part of a burgeoning fashion scene that's conquering wardrobes from New York to Japan.

And it's not just Stockholm threads stealing the headlines. A bold new wave of Michelin-star chefs has sexed up the city's food culture, redefining fusion and turning the Swedish capital into an unexpected epicentre of cutting-edge cuisine.

Not bad for a city already famed as a design heavyweight. In Stockholm, names like Thomas Sandell and Jonas Bohlin style everything from uberglam clubs to stainless-steel doorknobs. An even fresher league of talent is ditching the minimalist white of the 1990s, giving Stockholm bolder, more daring spaces to play in.

But don't think this passion for fashion implies a superficial soul. About 200 museums, art galleries and theatres pack the city, among them contemporary dance hothouse Dansens Hus and the mighty Moderna Museet, home to one of Europe's finest caches of 20th-century art. Pretty good for a city of 1.8 million on the geographic edge of the EU main stage.

So what's the catch? Admittedly, Stockholm is not cheap, but neither is New York or London. And as for those winter temperatures, with so many hotspots to hide in, who has time for counting centigrades (envious rivals aside)?

**Top left** Descending into Odenplan Tunnelbana station **Top right** See *God's Hand* by Carl Milles reaching for the sky at Millesgården (p19) **Bottom** Looking back at Stockholm from the island of Skeppsholmen (p76)

>HIGHLIGHTS

The cobbled streets of fairy-tale Gamla Stan (p10)

HIGHLIGHTS

# >1 GAMLA STAN

## EXPLORING THE LANES OF GAMLA STAN

Royal guards, sagging candy-coloured buildings and twisting cobbled lanes – Stockholm's Gamla Stan (Old Town) is a storybook wonderland. It's also the city's 11th-century birthplace, packed with historical anecdotes and crowd-pullers like royal palace Kungliga Slottet (p38) and the brilliantly offbeat Livrustkammaren (p38), home to royal swords, slippers and the stomach contents of a king's assassin.

Thankfully, most of the heavy tourism and souvenir hunting is concentrated along Västerlånggatan and Stora Nygatan, making it rather easy to avoid if you've no interest in ceramic Vikings, Dalahäst key chains or Absolut Swede shot glasses. Venture into the back alleys and you'll find a city that seems almost unchanged since medieval times. Here, leafy little squares hide dusty old shops and the only sound is your footsteps echoing down the street. It doesn't matter where you begin or where you end up – each corner seems to pack a surprise.

Make sure to pop into the beautiful Tyska Kyrkan (p41), Stockholm's 16th-century German church. If you're lucky, you'll catch the

KU-261-405

organist practising his Bach. If not, seek your own muse over a pot of Iranian tea at Chaikhana (p47). Close by sits Österlånggatan (Map p37, E4). For centuries one of Gamla Stan's busiest streets, it's now a laid-back strip of cute boutiques and artisan studios like eco-chic Ekovaruhuset (p42), ceramics workshop Gertrud Båge (p42) and the adorable kids' shop Kalikå (p43). It's also home to some fine Stockholm nosh-spots, including the crowd-pleasing Bistro Ruby (p44) and the shamelessly romantic Den Gyldene Freden (p45), nearly 290 years young and a perfect place for classic Swedish grub.

Predictably, history is something Gamla Stan does well. Its stalwart cathedral Storkyrkan (p41) hosted centuries of coronations while the picture-perfect square of Stortorget is the site of the gruesome 1520 Stockholm Bloodbath (see Background, p166), where 82 Swedish noblemen and citizens literally lost their heads. Of course, these days you're more likely to lose your head over one of the flirtatious waitstaff at Chokladkoppen (p47), where a summertime table on the square is a must for voyeurs in Gucci shades. If you can pull yourself away from sipping hot chocolates (or swapping numbers), don't miss dinner at turn-of-the-20th-century, Parisian-style Le Rouge (p47), home to two of Stockholm's hottest chefs and a red-velvety bar.

# >2 MODERNA MUSEET

## CULTURE AND KAFFE AT MODERNA MUSEET

The bad news: after a brief dabble with free admission, Moderna Museet (p79) is charging entrance fees again. The good news: Moderna Museet's killer modern-art collection is sharper than ever, including Paul McCarthy's outrageous installation *Ketchup Sandwich*, Dorothea Tanning's painting *Insomnias* and her foam-a-licious sculpture *Don Juan's Breakfast*. The Tanning acquisitions are part of the museum's ambitious Second Museum of Our Wishes project, which requested Skr50 million in government funding by 2008 to celebrate the museum's 50th anniversary by redressing the collection's gender imbalance.

Not that the museum is a stranger to enlightened thinking. In the 1960s, a then-fledgling gallery was already mingling with provocateurs like Andy Warhol, Jasper Johns and Niki de Saint Phalle, shaking up Sweden's conceptions of art and building up a contemporary collection now considered one of Europe's best. Warhol's first international retrospective was held here in 1968 and it was here that the world first heard his famously misquoted 'In the future everybody will be world famous for 15 minutes.' The Day-Glo cow wallpaper on the museum walls pays tribute to the show, in which Warhol wrapped the entire building in the stuff.

That building was the adjoining drill hall, Moderna Museet's original home and current abode of the Arkitekturmuseet (p78). Mould problems in the new museum building, designed by Spaniard Rafael Moneo, forced a two-year closure before a triumphant return to the space in 2004, complete with a sleek new espresso bar in the foyer (don't miss the nearby video station giving crucial background on temporary exhibitions) and revamped interiors in the well-stocked

## A DIFFERENT PERSPECTIVE

Aside from the free and enlightening audio guides, Moderna Museet occasionally runs thematic tours, including a Baby Tour for art buffs with bubs and a refreshing Queer Tour, which looks at the collection from a bent perspective. Tours cost Skr1000 per group. Contact the **gallery** ( ☎ 51 95 52 00; www.modernamuseet.se) for details.

museum shop and restaurant. Not that the restaurant needed nifty noise-reducing rubber tables to win fans – breathtaking views and an award-winning chef in the kitchen were more than adequate. In recent years, the restaurant has become a star in its own right, pulling in punters just for the food.

Not that we could ever do that. The art is too irresistible, with must-sees including Edward Kienholz's disturbing *The State Hospital*, Marcel Duchamp's *Fountain* and Salvador Dalí's cryptic *L'Enigme de Guillaume Tell*, which has kept Stockholmers debating its meaning for generations. Equally unmissable is the sheep-in-a-tyre creation *Monogram* by Robert Rauschenberg, whose long collaborative history with Moderna Museet saw a major retrospective of his work in 2007 and his handwritten scrawl turned into the museum's official logo.

# >3 SWEDISH DESIGN

## HUNTING DOWN CULT SWEDISH DESIGN

Stockholmers rattle off the names of designers the way Angelenos rattle on about botox. Here design is not frivolous; it's de rigueur. From tables to threads, designers are deities and designer stores are their temples. Begin your pilgrimage in the strictly stylish district of Östermalm (p108), home to classic design store Svenskt Tenn (p117). Close by, Sibyllegatan (Map pp110–11, C4) is lined with cult decorative art and furniture showrooms, among them Modernity (pictured above; p116), where the collection of 20th-century chairs, tables, vases and jewellery is the talk of Manhattan.

Further north in Vasastaden, forage through the antique shops on Upplandsgatan (Map pp52–3, D2) for retro lamps, or pop into nearby Platina (p63) for avant-garde Swedish bling from the likes of Agnieszka Knap and Annika Åkerfelt.

Less trodden but worth the trip is Kungsholmen (p126), home to the sprawling interior-design complex ROOM (p131), forward-thinking Frank Form (p129) and quirky design quartet Defyra (p129).

Across the waters of Riddarfjärden, Södermalm (p86) is the city's artistic epicentre, home to artisan co-ops and Swedish design icon 10 Swedish Designers (p93). For fresh new Scandi talent, don't miss DesignTorget (p94), where you're bound to catch the odd rising star flogging their next-wave wares.

# >4 ÖSTERMALMS SALUHALL

## SCOFFING DOWN SWEDISH DELICACIES AT ÖSTERMALMS SALUHALL

Östermalms Saluhall (p113) is not so much a food market as a gastronomic event. Best experienced at lunch on a Friday or Saturday, its exquisite *fin-de-siècle* stalls flaunt the country's finest foodstuffs, from just-in Nordic lobsters to cumin-spiced cheeses, succulent cloudberries and handmade champagne truffles. The scent of crushed coffee beans fills the air and the constant throng of fans includes old-money dames, celebrity chefs and the odd Swedish royal, known to drop by to stock the palace pantry.

Yet despite its high-class tendencies, this temple of fine food is a sublimely cosy affair. It's not unusual for traders to have worked at competing stalls, regular customers keep tabs, and a simple seafood question can easily turn into a lively conversation about the perfect herring. Indeed, whiling away an hour in here is perfectly justified. The espresso at Robert's Coffee would satisfy a Neapolitan, the fruit and vegetable displays could hang in the Tate and the lip-smacking selection of gourmet Scandi treats will have your tummy rumbling wantonly…in which case a serve of toast *skagen* (white toast topped with dilled shrimp mayonnaise and clouds of bleak roe) at Lisa Elmqvist (p119) should hit the spot.

And then there's always the building, a soaring concoction of red-brick spires and trés-chic ironwork by Isak Gustav Clason, famed architect of the Nordiska Museet (p79).

## >5 STOCKHOLM BY BALLOON

**FLOAT OVER STOCKHOLM AT 1000FT**

If you've ever envied Karlsson's magic flights over Stockholm in Astrid Lindgren's tale, book yourself a hot-air balloon for the next-best thing. From 1000ft, the Swedish capital oozes fairy-tale appeal – picture princely turrets, gingerbread townhouses and the navy-blue Baltic weaving its way around thousands of islands.

Ballooning tours operate from May to the end of September. They cost between Skr995 and Skr2000, and will see you up, up and away for about an hour. The entire arrangement, however, can last up to five hours, usually ending with a traditional champagne blessing for virgin balloonists, and picnic snacks for a postflight linger. Best of all, the long summer twilight not only makes evening ballooning possible, it makes it a must.

Predictably, such glowing views are highly coveted, so it's best to book a flight a month in advance. Pack the binoculars and don't forget to check the tour operator's policy on flight cancellations, as trips can never be confirmed until the actual day of flying…something Karlsson never had to worry about. For tour companies, see p183.

# >6 DJURGÅRDEN

## WINDING DOWN ON DJURGÅRDEN

Most metropolises would kill for Djurgården. Only minutes from downtown Norrmalm, its wooded parklands, grassy knolls and happily grazing sheep provide a soothing tonic for frazzled urbanites.

In fact, for inner-city natives, this central city island is the magic garden they never had – one with soaring forests, secret swimming spots and the odd royal palace. Waterside paths make for perfect jogs and bike rides, while the rambling tracks make for long soulful strolls, punctuated by the odd cosy cafe or intimate restaurant.

This one-time royal hunting ground is now part of Stockholm's Ekoparken, a sprawling greenbelt labelled the world's first urban national park. It boasts some of Europe's finest forests of giant oak and is home to Scandinavia's densest population of tawny owls.

Almost as dense is the number of must-see museums and attractions on the island, which include alfresco Skansen (p80), whimsical Junibacken (p78), vintage funpark Gröna Lund Tivoli (p85) and the sock-knocking Vasamuseet (p81), home of the 17th-century warship flop, the *Vasa*. And if museum fatigue sets in, you'll never be short of a peaceful place to stop, drop and chill.

# >7 KONDITORI TOUR

## LET THEM EAT CAKE

It's lucky Stockholm has so many nice running trails and bike paths – the readily available exercise makes it easier to indulge in one of the city's best-loved traditions, namely, eating cake. The Swedish habit of *fika* – to enjoy a drink and snack, usually coffee and cake, during a midafternoon break – may have grown from the abundance of awesome bakeries *(konditori)* that dot every neighbourhood. Gorgeous confections of cardamom and marzipan line up under glass cases, looking almost too pretty to eat – but not quite.

The city's traditional bakeries are numerous and evenly distributed. Though its decor has been modernised somewhat, the baked goodies at Thelins Konditori (p134) on Kungsholmen remain deliciously traditional. In Gamla Stan, don't miss the chance to pig out for charity at Grillska Husets Konditori (p45), the bakery run by the charity organisation Stockholms Stadsmission. Östermalm boasts the absolutely mammoth cinnamon rolls *(kanelbullar)* on offer at Café Saturnus (p118). And for high art in the baking department, seek out Xoko (p62), whose chef, Magnus Johansson, has done the desserts for the Nobel Prize feasts for the past several years.

# >8 MILLESGÅRDEN

## SOAKING UP SCULPTURE AND SUN AT MILLESGÅRDEN

Millesgården (see boxed text, p118) is the former home and studio of Carl Milles (1875–1955), one of Sweden's greatest sculptors. Perched on a cliff on the leafy island of Lidingö, the property's star attraction is its sublime sculpture garden, a breathtaking combo of fountains, terraces and sparkling views over the waters of Värtan.

Best of all, it's generously sprinkled with the bronzed works of Milles, including a replica of his enormous Poseidon statue in Gothenburg (1930). Sun or snow, a stroll through the grounds, watching Milles' whimsical figures balancing against the sky, is deliciously ethereal. More originals and replicas fill the artist's Italianate palazzo, which also houses Milles' impressive private art collection, from Hellenic sculpture and Etruscan figurines to Italian Renaissance paintings. The Little Studio features works by Milles' wife Olga (1874–1967) and elder sister Ruth (1873–1941), while a stunningly minimalist gallery designed by Johan Celsing serves up fresh new work from local and global artists.

# >9 STOCKHOLM ARCHIPELAGO

**CRUISING THE STOCKHOLM ARCHIPELAGO AT 45 KNOTS**

The archipelago is Stockholmers' favourite summer playground – a sublimely beautiful wonderland of cool Baltic waters, pine-brushed islands and cute summer cottages. While a steamboat tour offers a satisfactory introduction, way more exhilarating is a rip-roaring ride on a RIB (rigid inflatable boat). These sexy rubber beasts will have you flying across the water at up to 45 knots, which means more ground covered, more sea spray (don't fret, waterproof gear is provided) and an adrenalin rush that will leave you grinning for days. RIB Sightseeing (p183) runs 90-minute tours from mid-May to early September. Departing outside the National Museum, you'll zip past sights like garden island Djurgården (p17), ex-royal villa Prins Eugens Waldemarsudde (p80) and the hulking bulk of Vaxholm Kastell (p139). Thankfully, you'll be having too much fun to give a damn about the bad hair day waiting at the end.

# >STOCKHOLM DIARY

Stockholmers celebrate their seasons with passion. It's hardly surprising. After months of icy dark nights, locals pounce on spring with a biological urgency. Bonfires burn, shades are slipped on and denizens catch up on warmer Nordic sun. By summer, the party vibe hits high gear. Long languid days set the scene for twilight jazz, midnight marathons and sparkly pride parading. Shorter autumn days see film and poetry take the stage, while winter's gloom is lit up with candlelit processions, Christmas markets and adrenalin-pumped hockey playoffs. For the complete lowdown, check the tourist board's free monthly magazine *What's On – Stockholm*, or click onto www.stockholmtown.com.

Stockholmers love summer days in Djurgården (p17)

# FEBRUARY

## LG Hockey Games

www.swehockey.se

Hardcore hockey and harder-core fans make this four-nation fight for the Globen Cup a midwinter adrenalin rush.

## Stockholm Furniture Fair

www.stockholmfurniturefair.com

Star of Stockholm Design Week, this five-day furniture expo is open to mere mortals on the last day, usually a Sunday in mid-February. The fair is a big draw, so plan ahead; many of Stockholm's hotels will be booked solid.

## Market

www.market-art.se

Stockholm's newest art show collaborates with some of Scandinavia's hottest galleries. Expect a super-fine collection of contemporary Nordic and international works.

## Popcorn

www.popcorn.nu

Stockholm's other film festival is all about indie flicks, uberhip locations and film-themed club nights.

## Vikingarännet

www.vikingarännet.com

This immensely popular 80km ice-skating race in February starts in Uppsala, ends in Stockholm, and is open to everyone; fees are Skr400 to Skr600.

# MARCH

## Melodifestivalen

www.globearenas.se

The grand final of Scandinavia's campest song comp sees 10 acts battle it out to represent Sweden at the Eurovision Song Contest.

# APRIL

## Stockholm Filmfestivalen Junior

www.filmfestivalen.se

A junior version of the Stockholm International Film Festival, this week-long event screens stimulating flicks for film buffs aged six to 16.

## Valborgsmässoafton (Walpurgis Night)

www.skansen.se

On 30 April, snow-weary Swedes finally say 'Hej' to spring with bonfires, choirs and bizarre old-school games like 'Bat the Cat Out of the Vat'.

# MAY

## La Mayonnaise Open

www.mayo.se in Swedish

Not just for old French men, the largest boules competition in northern Europe pulls the hip and the hangers-on for multilevel tournaments and continental chilling on Långholmen island.

## Scandinavian Music Convention

www.aboutsmc.com

Hit the decks at this two-day dance-music convention in May. Events include kick-ass club nights and free workshops by big-name local and international DJs.

## Skärgårdsmarknad

www.stockholmtown.com

On the last weekend in May, traders from the archipelago descend on Djurgården to sell island produce and handicrafts, dish up archipelago delicacies and convince you to hit their turf.

## Stockholm Marathon

www.stockholmmarathon.se

In late May or early June, some 17,500 masochists sweat it out on one of world's most beautiful marathon circuits, taking in 42km of waterways, parks and city icons.

## Tjejtrampet

www.tjejtrampet.com in Swedish

The world's biggest women-only bicycle race sees young, old, professional and amateur slip on the Lycra for the picture-perfect 42km course.

## Smaka På Stockholm

www.smakapastockholm.se

In late May/early June, some 650,000 foodies blissfully nibble and sip at this six-day celebration of Stockholm's food scene, which includes cooking duels between the city's A-list chefs.

# JUNE

## Archipelago Boat Day

www.skargardstrafikanten.se

In early June, a fleet of old steamboats and other antique vessels go on parade from Stockholm's Strömkajen to Vaxholm, with parties at either end of the trip.

## Nationaldag

www.skansen.se

Sweden's national day boasts a parade and a traditionally clad king handing out Swedish flags at Skansen.

Sweaty joggers brave the Stockholm Marathon

STOCKHOLM DIARY

Festive flags fly for Nationaldag (p23)

### Midsummer's Eve

www.skansen.se

The first Friday after 21 June is Midsummer's Eve, when trad-clad Swedes raise the mid-summer pole to dance around, eat pickled herring and knock back snaps.

### Stockholm Pride Week

www.stockholmpride.org

In late July/early August, Stockholm goes pink with five fab days of queer parties, cultural events and Scandinavia's biggest gay pride parade.

## JULY

### Stockholm Summer Games

www.summergames.se

Held in Stockholm's 1912 Olympic stadium, this sports competition for youth features all the standard track and field events.

### Stockholm Jazz Festival

www.stockholmjazz.com

Five smooth days and nights of jazz, blues, soul and more from A-list guests like Kanye West and Stevie Wonder.

## AUGUST

### Archipelago Raid

www.archipelagoraid.com

Held in August, this extreme sailing race is set around 100,000 precarious rocks and islands of the Stockholm archipelago, attracting thrillseekers from across the world.

### Stockholms Kulturfestival

www.kulturfestivalen.stockholm.se

One buzzing week of everything (and anything) from sidewalk opera to street theatre, dance gigs and off-beat walking tours, with most of the 400-odd cultural events absolutely free.

## Midnattsloppet (Midnight Run)
www.midnattsloppet.com
A Stockholm institution, this 10km nocturnal dash through Södermalm is a pounding spectacle of 20,000 runners and 200,000 spectators, as well as curbside Samba partying.

# SEPTEMBER
## Stockholm Beer & Whisky Festival
www.stockholmbeer.se in Swedish
For two weekends in late September (and early October), this beachside bev fest entertains with tastings, exhibitions, and beer and whisky schools in what is one of the world's biggest and best booze-ups.

# OCTOBER
## Hem
www.stockholmsmassan.se/hem
Get clued-up on the latest Nordic trends at Sweden's biggest home and interior design show. Held in October, it stars celebrity renovators and 85,000 design-obsessed Swedes.

## Stockholm Open
www.stockholmopen.se
Nine days of international tennis and courtside celebrity-spotting in a tournament organised by on-court legend Sven Davidson.

# NOVEMBER
## Stockholm Poetry Festival
www.00tal.com
Artists, thinkers and hopeless romantics converge at the lavish Kungliga Dramatiska Teatern (Royal Dramatic Theatre, p123) to watch poetry merge with music, dance and performance art.

## Stockholm International Film Festival
www.filmfestivalen.se
When Quentin Tarantino says it's good, who's to disagree? This 10-day flickfest features 170 films from 40 countries, screened in cinemas across town.

### QUIRKY HOLIDAYS
**Skärgårdsbåtens Dag** On Archipelago Boat Day, held on the first Wednesday in June, a parade of old-fashioned steamboats sails from Strömkajen (in Stockholm) to Vaxholm, where they're met with folk dancing, a market and giddy summer merriment.
**Luciadagen** On 13 December, young girls wear flames on their heads in honour of St Lucia, delivering saffron bread to adoring parents.

STOCKHOLM DIARY

# DECEMBER

## Christmas Markets

www.skansen.se

Get into the festive vibe, or at least the *glögg* (mulled wine) and ginger snaps at Skansen, home to Stockholm's biggest Yuletide market. The main Christmas holiday in Sweden is Julafton (Christmas Eve) on 24 December.

## Nyårsafton

www.skansen.se

Skansen's New Year's Eve bash is broadcast live on Swedish TV, from the traditional reading of Tennyson's 'Ring Out, Wild Bells' to the final thrilling fireworks extravaganza.

Catching some rays at Rosendals Trädgård (p84)

# ITINERARIES

Clean and compact, Stockholm makes for hassle-free urban ambling. One minute you're channelling your inner bohemian in Södermalm, the next you're shopping for caviar at an Östermalm market. Done, you can hop on a ferry, hide in a forest and still be back in time for oysters *Fine de Claire* in a converted Kungsholmen factory. See also Organised Tours (p183).

## ONE DAY

Start where Stockholm itself began – Gamla Stan (p36). Explore the back-lanes, watch St George wrestle the dragon inside Storkyrkan (p41) and catch the Changing of the Guard outside Kungliga Slottet (see boxed text, p38). From Slussen, catch the ferry to Skeppsholmen for wasabi and Warhol at Moderna Museet (p12) before trekking to SoFo (p94) for afternoon shopping. Watch the sun set from Katarinahissen (p91) before dinner and drinks at Allmänna Galleriet 925 (p132).

## THREE DAYS

Follow the one-day itinerary before dropping into the Vasamuseet (p81) and open-air Skansen (p80). Lunch at Lisa På Udden (p84), then hire a kayak (p85). If there's time, pop into Birger Jarlspassagen (p115) for a wardrobe overhaul before bagging a pavement table at Sturehof (p119) for dinner. Saunter on to Nox (p121) or catch some jazz at Jazzclub Fasching (p73). The following day, cruise the archipelago (p20) before a little late-night hedonism at Berns Salonger (p72), Cocktail Club @ Grodan Grev Ture (p123) or Marie Laveau (p106).

## WINTER WONDERLAND WEEKEND

Warm up with brunch at Grands Veranda (p67), shop for angora mittens at NK (p62) then skate a figure-eight at Kungsans Isbana (p74). Slurp soup at Sibiriens Soppkök (p70), curl up on a couch inside Kulturhuset's reading room (p56) or soak and steam at Sturebadet (p125). Tuck into meatballs and beer at Pelikan (p102) before catching some tunes at Pet Sounds (p104). The following morning, ramble through the woods of Djurgården (p17), ending up at cosy Rosendals Trädgård (p84) for

**Top left** Across the water from the National Museum (p56) **Top right** Fashion frenzy: Mrs H at Birger Jarlspassagen (p115) **Bottom** Meet your meat at Hötorgshallen market (p68)

lunch. Spend the afternoon at the brooding Armémuseum (p109) before therapeutic lounging at Iglo Ljuscafé (see boxed text, p99). If there's time, enjoy a warm skinny-dip at Liljeholmsbadet (p106) before tropical Thai at Koh Phangan (p101) and a sweaty gig at Debaser (p105) or Mosebacke Etablissement (p106).

## STOCKHOLM ON A PLATE

Start with some perfect pastries at Café Saturnus (p118), then pop into Östermalms Saluhall (p15). Then bag a Swedish cookbook at NK (p62) before lunch at Lux Stockholm (p133). Pick up designer crockery at Konsthantverkana (p97) and local tea at Tea Centre of Stockholm (p98). In late May to early June, don't miss Smaka På Stockholm (p23). Otherwise, opt for cocoa at Chokladfabriken (p94) before some top-notch noshing at Republik (p70), Esperanto (p65) or Edsbacka Krog (see boxed text, p65).

## SOMETHING FOR NOTHING

Begin your day of price-less pleasure at Stadsbiblioteket (p57). Amble across to Gustav Vasa Kyrkan (p55), eye-up the art at Brändström & Stene

### FORWARD PLANNING

**Three to six months before you go** If you're visiting in March, bag yourself tickets to the Melodifestivalen final (see boxed text, p85). Book a chocolate-tasting session at Chokladfabriken (p94) and scan www.ticnet.se for sports and entertainment events.

**Two months before you go** Check out the websites for Dansens Hus (p73), Folkoperan (p105), Kungliga Dramatiska Teatern (p123) and Strindbergs Intimateater (p75) for upcoming shows.

**Three to four weeks before you go** Top-notch restaurants like Leijontornet (p47) and Operakällaren (p69) should be booked around now, as well as a Sunday-night table at Lady Patricia (p106). Book a hot-air balloon flight (p183).

**Two weeks before you go** Book a spa treatment at Sturebadet (p125) or Yasuragi (see boxed text, p120), check www.stockholmtown.com for current exhibitions, and check the homepages of Cocktail Club @ Grodan Grev Ture (p123), Mosebacke Etablissement (p106) and Debaser (p105) for upcoming gigs.

**A few days before you go** Book a table at Allmänna Galleriet 925 (p132) and Republik (p70). Scan www.nojesguiden.se and www.dn.se (both in Swedish) for culture-scene updates. Check www.biljettnu.se for tickets to sold-out events and email nightclubs like Laroy (p124) and Berns Salonger (p72) to get on the guestlist.

(p54), then head to Hötorgshallen (p68) for free tastings. If it's August, check out Stockholms Kulturfestival (p24). If not, investigate Kulturhuset (p56), then kick back on a square in Gamla Stan (p36) and start on that Strindberg novel.

## DESIGN & THE CITY

Head out to Skogskyrkogården (see boxed text, p49), then back in for the National Museum (p56) or Arkitekturmuseet (p78). Lunch at Freds-gatan 12 (p67), then hunt down classic Swedish design at Svenskt Tenn (p117) and Modernity (p116). Alternatively, explore the streets of Söder-malm for gems like DesignTorget (p94), 10 Swedish Designers (p93) and Blås & Knåda (p93). Hobnob with designers at Svensk Form (p81), then nosh and relax at designer dining dens Landet (see boxed text, p84) or Kungsholmen (p132).

>NEIGHBOURHOODS

The lights of the old city, Gamla Stan (p36)

NEIGHBOURHOODS

# NEIGHBOURHOODS

Built on 14 islands connected by 57 bridges, Stockholm is a glittering show-off. While there's no doubting its knockout natural assets, they're easily matched by Stockholm's deliciously contrasting neighbourhoods.

The city's historic and geographic heart is Gamla Stan (Old Town), a cosy concoction of medieval squares, 17th-century merchants' houses and barrel-vaulted cafes. This is the place to stock up on reindeer skins, kick back on fairy-tale squares and snoop around royal apartments.

Just a quick stumble to the north, Norrmalm slaps you in the face with its bumper-to-bumper traffic, post-war office blocks and sprawling retail temples. Never a philistine, it's also home to cultural classics like the National Museum, Konserthuset and art-jammed Kulturhuset.

Further north, residential Vasastaden provides a satisfying slice of daily life – think antiques stores, buzzing bars, fresh local galleries and too-cute bookstores. To the west, up-and-coming Kungsholmen sports an even more neighbourly vibe. Here, conversation comes with your semla bun, and your waitress probably worked at the quirky vintage shop across the street…the one where the owner hand-paints your shopping bag.

East of it all lies Östermalm, with its Prada-proud fashionistas, cult design stores, lobster lunches and celebrity-laced clubbing. South of these mon-eyed streets is Djurgården, sprinkled with forests, a fun park and Stockholm's museum heavyweights. Wedged between Djurgården and Gamla Stan, Skeppsholmen is also culturally well endowed, home to modern art hotspot Moderna Museet and the Eastern exotica of Östasiatiska Museet.

Yet the biggest and possibly best of the lot is the island of Södermalm. South of Gamla Stan, this is where Stockholm gets down indie-style with cutting-edge fashion, bohemian bars and verve in its vegan veins.

Further out, suburban Stockholm harbours some hidden gems, from the pine-brushed beauty of Skogskyrkogården in the south to Milles-gården's whimsical sculpture garden to the north. Topping it all off is the Stockholm archipelago, a dreamy combo of sea, sky, rock and wish-they-were-mine yachts.

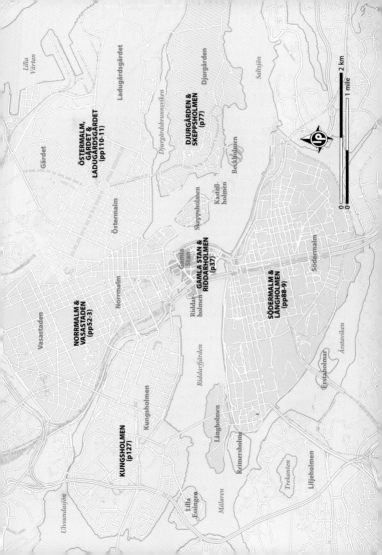

Lilla Värtan

Laddugårdsgärdet

Djurgården

Saltsjön

Gärdet

Djurgårdsbrunnsviken

**ÖSTERMALM, GÄRDET & LADUGÅRDSGÄRDET (pp110–11)**

**DJURGÅRDEN & SKEPPSHOLMEN (p77)**

Östermalm

Skeppsholmen

Kastell-holmen

Beckholmen

0 2 km
0 1 mile

**NORRMALM & VASASTADEN (pp52–3)**

Normalm

Gamla Stan

**GAMLA STAN & RIDDARHOLMEN (p37)**

Vasastaden

Riddar-holmen

Södermalm

**SÖDERMALM & LÅNGHOLMEN (pp88–9)**

Riddarfjärden

**KUNGSHOLMEN (p127)**

Kungsholmen

Långholmen

Reimersholme

Erstaholmen

Årstaviken

Ulvsundasjön

Lilla Essingen

Mälaren

Trekanten

Liljeholmen

# >GAMLA STAN & RIDDARHOLMEN

Gamla Stan (Old Town; p10) is Stockholm's undisputed heart stealer. Disorientating lanes twist past Renaissance churches, baroque palaces and romantic squares. These cobblestones have seen it all, from triumphant kings on horseback to bloody mass beheadings. Little more than a century ago, a crumbling Gamla Stan was itself condemned to death by Stockholm's slum-slashing city planners. Thankfully, high-profile protesters like August Strindberg and Carl Larsson set them straight, and by the 1960s Gamla Stan was precious protected property.

Separated from Gamla Stan by a slender canal, desolate Riddarholmen (Island of Knights) – named because the 17th-century knights who served in the Thirty Years' War were given palaces here – is home to the striking iron-spired church, Riddarholmskyrkan, and one resident family.

Even tinier is speck-of-an-island Helgeandsholmen. Wedged between Gamla Stan and Norrmalm, it's home to the Swedish parliament building, Riksdagshuset, and its cool-tempered debates.

## GAMLA STAN & RIDDARHOLMEN

### ◎ SEE

| | | |
|---|---|---|
| Gustav III's Antikmuseum | 1 | D1 |
| Kungliga Myntkabinettet | 2 | E2 |
| Kungliga Slottet (Royal Palace) | 3 | D2 |
| Livrustkammaren | 4 | E2 |
| Museum Tre Kronor | 5 | D1 |
| Nobelmuseet | 6 | D2 |
| Parliament Building Tours Entrance | 7 | C1 |
| Postmuseum | 8 | C3 |
| Riddarholmskyrkan | 9 | B3 |
| Riddarhuset | 10 | C2 |
| Riksdagshuset | 11 | C1 |
| Royal Palace Information Office & Bookshop | 12 | D2 |
| Skattkammaren | 13 | D2 |
| Storkyrkan | 14 | D2 |
| Tyska Kyrkan | 15 | D3 |

### ⌂ SHOP

| | | |
|---|---|---|
| Castor Konsthantverk | 16 | E3 |
| Ekovaruhuset | 17 | E3 |
| Gertrud Båge | 18 | E3 |
| Got to Hurry | 19 | D3 |
| Kalikå | 20 | E3 |
| Mode Rosa | 21 | D3 |
| Själagårdsbodarna | 22 | E3 |
| Sweden Bookshop | 23 | E2 |
| Systembolaget | 24 | D4 |

### ⑪ EAT

| | | |
|---|---|---|
| Bistro Ruby | (see 27) | |
| Café Art | 25 | D3 |
| Den Gyldene Freden | 26 | E4 |
| Grill Ruby | 27 | E2 |
| Grillska Husets Konditori | 28 | D2 |
| Hermitage | 29 | C3 |
| Le Rouge | 30 | E2 |
| Leijontornet | 31 | C3 |

### ▼ DRINK

| | | |
|---|---|---|
| Chaikhana | 32 | D3 |
| Chokladkoppen | 33 | D3 |
| Kaffekoppen | (see 33) | |
| Torget | 34 | C3 |
| Wirströms Pub | 35 | C2 |

### ★ PLAY

| | | |
|---|---|---|
| Lino | 36 | C3 |
| Stampen | 37 | C2 |

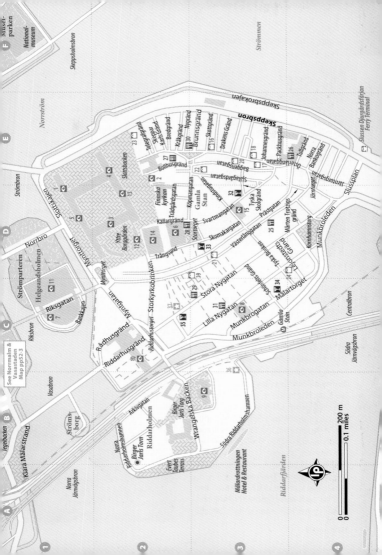

NEIGHBOURHOODS

GAMLA STAN & RIDDARHOLMEN

# SEE

## KUNGLIGA MYNTKABINETTET

☎ 51 95 53 14; www.myntkabinettet
.se; Slottsbacken 6; adult/under 18yr/
concession Skr50/free/30, Stockholm Card
free, Mon free; ☼ 10am-4pm Oct-Jun,
9am-5pm Jul-Sep; Ⓜ Gamla Stan; ♿
Anything but a dreary accountant's
fantasy, the fabulous Royal Coin
Cabinet sparkles with a priceless
collection of world-turning currency, including Viking silver and
the world's oldest coin (created
in Greece in 625 BC), as well as its
heaviest (a copper plate weighing
19.7kg). The exhibitions are innovative, the kids' playroom is fun and
the kitsch collection of piggy-banks
alone is worth the trip.

## KUNGLIGA SLOTTET

☎ 402 61 30; www.kungahuset.se;
Slottsbacken; adult/child Skr100/50,
Stockholm Card free; ☼ 10am-5pm Jun-
Aug, noon-3pm Sep-May; Ⓜ Gamla Stan
Built on the ruins of the original
Tre Kronor royal fortress, this 18th-
century palace has 608 rooms and
three museums: the Skattkammaren
(Royal Treasury; ☼ free 45min tours in English
2pm Tue & Thu Feb–mid-May, 2pm daily
mid-May–mid-Sep), the archeologically
inclined Museum Tre Kronor (☼ free
tours in English noon mid-May–mid-Sep) and
the hit-and-miss Gustav III's Antikmu-
seum (☼ free tours in English daily 2pm, also

4pm Jun-Aug). Upstaging them all are
the Royal Apartments, dripping
in rococo excess and home to the
decadent Karl XI Gallery, inspired
by Versailles' Hall of Mirrors and
considered the finest example
of Swedish late baroque. They're
best tackled with a free guided tour
( ☼ in English 2pm Wed-Sun Feb–mid-May,
11am, 1pm, 3pm mid-May–mid-Sep), which
gives the lowdown on some rather
kooky royal behaviour. A combination ticket (adult/child Skr130/65) admits
you to the Royal Apartments,
museums and Royal Chapel.

## LIVRUSTKAMMAREN

☎ 51 95 55 44; www.livrustkammaren
.se; Slottsbacken 3, Kungliga Slottet;
adult/under 18yr Skr60/free, Stockholm
Card free; ☼ 11am-5pm Tue, Wed &
Fri-Sun, to 8pm Thu Sep-Apr, 11am-5pm
Tue-Sun May, 10am-5pm daily Jun-Aug;
Ⓜ Gamla Stan

## POMP 'N' PARADE

For a fix of royal pomp, don't miss the
Changing of the Guard in the outer
western courtyard of the Royal Palace.
With camper hats and arguably cuter
guards than its British counterpart, this
regal ritual takes place at 12.15pm Monday to Saturday and 1.15pm Sunday and
public holidays May to August, 12.15pm
Wednesday and Saturday and 1.15pm
Sunday April and September to October,
noon Wednesday and Saturday and 1pm
Sunday November to March.

Nobel winners inspire visitors at the Nobelmuseet

Quite frankly, the Royal Armoury Museum is brilliant. A regal storage attic of sorts, its engrossing collection of booty spans over 500 years of royal childhoods, coronations, weddings and murders. Sneak a peek at lavish royal wardrobes, King Gustav III's masquerade costume (worn when he was shot in 1792) and the preserved stomach contents of Baron Bielke, one of the conspirators to the king's assassination.

### NOBELMUSEET
☎ 53 48 18 00; www.nobelmuseum.se; Börshuset, Stortorget; adult/under 7yr/child/concession Skr60/free/20/40, Stockholm Card free; ⏱ 11am-8pm Tue & to 5pm Wed-Sun mid-Sep–mid-May, 10am-5pm & to 8pm Tue mid-May–mid-Sep; Ⓜ Gamla Stan; ♿
More about ideas and inspiration than artefacts, the minimalist Nobelmuseet features some fascinating short films on the theme of 'creativity', an audio archive of acceptance speeches, interviews with and readings from laureates like Martin Luther King and Ernest Hemingway, and cafe chairs signed by the visiting prize winners (turn them over to see!). To get the most out of the museum, join a free **guided tour** ( ⏱ in English 11.15am & 3pm Mon-Fri, 11.15am & 4pm Sat & Sun).

### POSTMUSEUM
☎ 781 17 59; www.postmuseum.posten.se; Lilla Nygatan 6; adult/under 18yr/concession Skr50/free/40, Stockholm Card free; ⏱ 11am-4pm Tue-Sun, to 7pm Wed; Ⓜ Gamla Stan; ♿
While a museum dedicated to almost four centuries of Swedish postal history sounds positively mind-numbing, Stockholm's Post Museum is surprisingly engrossing, crammed with old mail

carriages, a climb-aboard train carriage, offbeat postcards and a cute children's post office downstairs for budding postal workers. Previous temporary exhibitions have covered everything from the life of the Great Garbo to the kiss in art.

### RIDDARHOLMSKYRKAN

☎ 402 61 30; www.royalcourt.se; Birger Jarls Torg; adult/under 7yr/concession Skr30/free/15; ⏰ 10am-4pm mid-May–late May & early Sep–mid-Sep, 10am-5pm Jun-Aug; M Gamla Stan

With its dramatic iron spire stabbing at the sky, Riddarholmskyrkan (on Riddarholmen) is a Stockholm icon. Built by Franciscan monks in the late 13th century and expanded in the mid-15th century, it has been the final resting place of Swedish monarchs since the burial of the mighty Gustav II Adolf in 1632; his marble sarcophagus lies in the Gustavian chapel.

### RIDDARHUSET

☎ 723 39 90; www.riddarhuset .se; Riddarhustorget 10; adult/ concession Skr50/25, Stockholm Card free; ⏰ 11.30am-12.30pm Mon-Fri; M Gamla Stan

Admirers of architecture shouldn't miss this 17th-century Dutch baroque masterpiece, designed by Simon de la Vallée, Heinrich Wilhelm, Joost Vingboons and Jean de la Vallée. Used by the Swedish parliament between 1641 and 1674, it still hosts the triennial Assembly of Nobles. While the chancellery houses some 300 pieces of heraldic porcelain, the real scene-stealer is the Great Hall, plastered with 2345 coats of arms belonging to Swedish nobility, as well as a precious ivory-carved land-marshall's chair from 1625 and a beautiful ceiling painting by 17th-century artist David Klöcker Ehenstrahl.

### WORTH THE TRIP

Despite Gamla Stan's regal vibe, it's the island of Lovön, 10km further west, that the Swedish royals call home. Here, their Unesco-listed **Drottningholms Slott** ( ☎ 402 62 80; www .kungahuset.se; adult/concession Skr70/30, combination ticket Skr90, chapel free; ⏰ 10am-4.30pm May-Aug, noon-3.30pm Sep, noon-3.30pm Sat & Sun Oct-Apr; M Brommaplan, then bus 301-323) is a wonderland of Renaissance-inspired palace, French-style gardens and the whimsical 18th-century **Drottningholms Slottsteater** (Court Theatre; ☎ 759 04 06; adult/7-18yr Skr60/free). The world's oldest theatre still in its original state, its summertime performances still use the vintage machinery. Equally unmissable is **Kina Slott** ( ☎ 402 62 70; adult/7-18yr Skr60/25; ⏰ 11am-4.30pm May-Aug, noon-3.30pm Tue-Sun Sep, noon-3.30pm Sat & Sun Oct-Apr), a lavishly decorated and skilfully restored Chinese pavilion (1753).

### RIKSDAGSHUSET

☎ 786 40 00; www.riksdagen.se; Riksgatan 3A; admission free; ⏱ 1hr guided tours in English 1.30pm Sat & Sun Sep–mid-Jun, noon, 1pm, 2pm & 3pm Mon-Fri mid-Jun–Aug; Ⓜ Kungsträdgården; ♿

It mightn't sound like the most exciting way to spend an hour, but tours of Sweden's parliament building are actually fascinating, taking in artworks by Otte Sköld and Axel Törneman, as well as Elisabet Hasselberg Olsson's *Memory of a Landscape*, a 54-sq-metre, 100kg tapestry woven in 200 shades of grey. The rather dreamy Swedish system of consensus-building, as presented by clued-up guides, has been known to elicit chuckles of disbelief.

### STORKYRKAN

☎ 723 30 00; Trångsund; adult/child Skr30/free, Stockholm Card free; ⏱ 9am-7pm mid-May–Aug, 9am-7pm Mon-Sat & 9am-5.30pm Sun Sep–mid-May; Ⓜ Gamla Stan

One-time venue of royal weddings and coronations, Stockholm's 700-year-old cathedral is also its oldest parish church. The Gothic-cum-baroque interior includes extravagant royal-box pews designed by Nicodemus Tessin the Younger and the famous Parhelion Painting, a 1630 copy of the earlier original depicting Stockholm during

an eerie display of atmospheric optics in 1535. The star attraction, however, is German Berndt Notke's dramatic Gothic sculpture *St George and the Dragon*, commissioned by Sten Sture the Elder to commemorate his victory over the Danes in 1471.

### TYSKA KYRKAN

☎ 411 11 88; Svartmangatan 16; admission free; ⏱ noon-4pm early May-late Sep, noon-4pm Sat & Sun late Sep-early May; Ⓜ Gamla Stan

Echoing back to the days of the Hanseatic League, when Stockholm and Germany shared tight trade links, the sublimely beautiful Tyska Kyrkan (German Church) dates from the 1570s, but was enlarged between 1638 and 1642. Highlights include a gilded royal gallery historically used for German members of the royal family, royal pews by Nicodemus Tessin the Elder, 119 unique gallery paintings (1660–65) and an astonishing ebony and alabaster pulpit (1660).

# SHOP

### CASTOR KONSTHANTVERK
*Handicrafts*

☎ 21 62 51; www.castorhantverk .com; Österlånggatan 27; ⏱ 11am-6pm Mon-Fri year-round, 11am-4pm Sat & Sun Jun-Sep; Ⓜ Gamla Stan

Sort of a one-stop shop for fine, high-quality handicrafts, this charming little store gathers work by a variety of different artists and craftspeople – you'll find everything from sheepskin hats and woven coats to unique jewellery and leather wristbands decorated with silver thread in the Sami (indigenous Scandinavian) tradition.

### EKOVARUHUSET
*Concept Store*
☎ 22 98 45; www.ekovaruhuset.se; Österlånggatan 28; ⏰ 11am-6pm Mon-Fri, 11am-4pm Sat & Sun; Ⓜ Gamla Stan
With a sister shop in Manhattan, this enlightened fashion boutique stocks only fair trade, organic products, from cosmetics and chocolates to trendy clothes and

sneakers. Hard-to-find labels include Kuyichi denim from Holland, Veja volleyball shoes from France and no-fuss streetwear from Gothenburg label Dem Collective.

### GERTRUD BÅGE *Ceramics*
☎ 20 67 09; gertrudbage@home.se; Österlånggatan 39; ⏰ 11am-6pm Mon-Fri, noon-4pm Sat; Ⓜ Gamla Stan
No-nonsense Gertrud is one of Sweden's leading ceramicists, and her richly textured plates, bowls and vases make a refreshing change from white-on-white minimalism. Although you'll find her wares at design store Blås & Knåda (p93), this is her studio and where you're most likely to see her in action.

## SYSTEMBOLAGET
Sweden's tough stance on lowering alcohol consumption and alcohol-related illnesses sees the state-owned bottle-shop chain Systembolaget solely responsible for selling to the masses alcoholic beverages with an alcohol volume above 3.5%. According to the bureaucrats, curbing private profit from alcohol sales means a less competitive market and lower alcohol abuse. Even in the state-owned stores, discounts, two-for-one deals and preferential treatment of products is strictly prohibited. Nanny State or not, it seems to do the trick – Sweden has one of the lowest death rates from cirrhosis of the liver in Europe. Not that Systembolaget isn't 'with it' – in recent years, slick supermarket-style outlets have replaced the former queue-by-number shops and the stock is thirst-quenchingly impressive. Central outlets include:
**Gamla Stan** ( ☎ 411 65 06; Lilla Nygatan 18; ⏰ 10am-6pm Mon-Wed, 10am-7pm Thu & Fri, 10am-3pm Sat)
**Norrmalm** (Map pp52-3, E5; ☎ 21 47 44; Klarabergsgatan 62; ⏰ 10am-8pm Mon-Fri, 10am-3pm Sat)
**Södermalm** (Map pp88-9, B2; ☎ 669 71 05; Långholmsgatan 21; ⏰ 10am-6pm Mon-Wed, 10am-7pm Thu & Fri, 10am-3pm Sat)

### ☐ GOT TO HURRY *Music*
☎ 411 24 84; Yxsmedsgränd 4;
🕙 10am-6pm Mon-Fri, 10am-4pm Sat;
Ⓜ Gamla Stan

Hidden away down a skinny laneway, this tiny record store has a global reputation for stocking obscure and limited-edition CDs and '60s and '70s vinyl. Expect anything from California psychedelia to kitsch Italian pop and a Japanese edition of Led Zeppelin's *II* album.

### ☐ KALIKÅ
*Children's Toys & Clothes*
☎ 20 52 19; www.kalika.se; Österlånggatan 18; 🕙 10am-6pm Mon-Fri, to 4pm Sat & Sun; Ⓜ Gamla Stan

This wholesome toy shop sells adorable handmade soft toys, dolls and felt puppets made by the mothers of Russian children with disabilities. The program, entitled 'Fair Play', was set up to financially support women and prevent their children from ending up in Russian orphanages. You can also buy toy-making kits, cute kids' clothes and giant wooden pencils to infantilise your office.

### ☐ MODE ROSA *Hats*
☎ 10 58 85; www.moderosa.se;
Västerlånggatan 45; 🕙 11am-6pm
Tue-Fri, 11am-5pm Sat, noon-4pm Sun;
Ⓜ Gamla Stan

Rosa Langer started this tiny hat shop in 1940, a fact that's reflected

Swedish souvenirs

in the timeless quality and styles of the toppers on offer. In 2008 she handed over management of the shop to the next generation, who have added a few items of clothing to the repertoire, but it's still all about cute, cool and classy hats.

### ☐ SJÄLAGÅRDSBODARNA *Gifts*
☎ 20 25 00; Själagårdsgatan 7-9;
🕙 10am-6pm Mon-Fri, to 4pm Sat,
noon-4pm Sun; Ⓜ Gamla Stan

The shop that time thankfully forgot, this lovingly cluttered burrow belongs in a bedtime book. Squeeze your way in for cute knick-knacks like moose-shaped cookie cutters, pressed-tin trams and original 1920s bookmarks. Best of all, the affable owner will wrap it all up in *Emily the Terrible* gift wrap.

### ☐ SWEDEN BOOKSHOP *Books*
☎ 789 21 31; www.swedenbookshop.se; Slottsbacken 10; ☼ 10am-6pm Mon-Fri year-round, 10am-3pm Sat & Sun Jul & Aug; Ⓜ Gamla Stan

If you're after books on Sweden and Swedish culture, it's hard to beat this place. Part of the Swedish Institute, you'll find everything from luscious Bruno Mathsson design books to gripping crime

fiction by Henning Mankell. Books come in all major languages.

# 🍴 EAT

Despite the historic vibe, Gamla Stan harbours some edgy dining hotspots. Of course, old-school charm is also on the menu, with centuries-old restaurants and cosy candlelit cellars.

### 🍴 BISTRO RUBY & GRILL RUBY
*French/American*          €€€
☎ 20 60 15; www.bistroruby.com; Österlånggatan 14; ☼ brunch Sat, din-

Den Gyldene Freden

ner Bistro Ruby 5pm-midnight, Grill Ruby 5pm-1am; Ⓜ Gamla Stan
Looking très Français with its rich red walls and art-salon look, Bistro Ruby boasts Gallic-inspired dishes and a grown-up bar for civilised conversation. Next door, low-key Grill Ruby kicks back with tasty Tex-Mex grub, Big Mama Thornton on the stereo and big American brunches on Saturday from 1pm.

### 🍴 CAFÉ ART  *Cafe*  €
☎ 411 76 61; Västerlånggatan 60; 🕓 10am-9pm Mon-Thu, 11am-10pm Fri-Sun; Ⓜ Gamla Stan
This dark, atmospheric, barrel-vaulted cellar cranks up the cosy factor with its candlelit tables, snug dark nooks and art-slung walls. A perfect spot for *fika* (coffee and cake), it also makes a mean salami and brie baguette.

### 🍴 DEN GYLDENE FREDEN  *Swedish*  €€€
☎ 24 97 60; www.gyldenefreden.se; Österlånggatan 51; 🕓 11.30am-2pm & 5pm-midnight Mon-Fri, 1pm-midnight Sat; Ⓜ Gamla Stan
Simmering and stirring since 1722, this venerable barrel-vaulted restaurant is run by the Swedish Academy, where (rumour has it) its members meet to decide who will win the Nobel prize. Personally, we think it should go to the chefs, whose sublime offer-

ings include civilised *husmanskost* (traditional Swedish fare) such as smoked salmon with avocado crème, figs and raisin dressing. Book ahead and dress to impress.

### 🍴 GRILLSKA HUSETS KONDITORI  *Bakery/Cafe*  €
☎ 787 86 03; Stortorget 3; 🕓 10am-8pm; Ⓜ Gamla Stan
The cafe and bakery run by Stockholms Stadsmission, the chain of secondhand charity shops, is a top-notch spot for a sweet treat or a sandwich, especially when warm weather allows for seating at the outdoor tables in Gamla Stan's main square. Don't pass up the chance to try a *mumma,* one of the bakery's specialities, a decadent little egg-and-cardamom flavour bomb.

### 🍴 HERMITAGE  *Vegetarian*  €€
☎ 411 95 00; Stora Nygatan 11; 🕓 11am-8pm Mon-Sat, noon-4pm Sun; Ⓜ Gamla Stan; Ⓥ

### A TIGHT SQUEEZE
A mere 90cm wide, **Mårten Trotzigs gränd** (Map p37, D4) is Stockholm's narrowest laneway. Located off the southern end of Västerlånggatan, Moby fans will recall the singer running through it in his music video clip for the James Bond theme. The clip was directed by Stockholm's Jonas Åkerlund.

**Sara Arrhenius**
*Curator, Bonniers Konsthall*

**Describe the gallery?** Bonniers Konsthall (p54) is a gallery for emerging Swedish and international artists. We want to introduce the audience to new tendencies and ideas and to support new art. Aside from our exhibitions we run an intense program of talks, performances, concerts and guided tours. **What's the visual-arts scene like?** Stockholm is a great city for contemporary art! I think it is quite exceptional for a city of its size to have so many and diverse art institutions – independent spaces, commercial galleries, artist-run spaces, large institutions with a long history, like Moderna Museet (p12), but also new, privately founded places like Bonniers Konsthall and Magasin 3 (p112). Stockholm still is not a big city, so the art scene has a quite open, informal character with an interesting exchange between contemporary art and the music, dance, fashion and design scenes. **Where can visitors see work by up-and-coming artists?** The new gallery area on Hudiksvallsgatan close to Bonniers Konsthall is a great place to start. On opening nights, especially warm evenings in August, it's like a moving outdoor cocktail party. Perfect to get to know the scene and to get involved!

All hail herbivorous Hermitage, famed for its cosy laid-back vibe and soulful veggie fare. Everyone from Stockholm students to frazzled tourists comes here for global flavours like spicy Moroccan stews and creamy cottage cheese pancakes. Indecisive types can opt for a bit of everything, served high and mighty on a gut-filling plate.

### LE ROUGE French €€€

☎ 50 52 44 30; Österlånggatan 17; ⏱ 11.30am-2pm & 5pm-1am Mon-Thu, 11.30am-2pm & 4pm-1am Fri, 5pm-1am Sat; Ⓜ Gamla Stan

The plush red velvet interior and French bistro grub at this relative newcomer to Stockholm's Old Town recall *fin de siècle* Paris. Run by two of Stockholm's hottest chefs, Melker Andersson and Danyel Couet, the restaurant's luxe French and Italian dishes are complemented by fancy drinks and DJs on most nights in the adjoining bar.

### LEIJONTORNET
New Swedish €€€

☎ 50 64 00 80; www.leijontornet.se; Lilla Nygatan 5; ⏱ 6-10pm Mon-Sat; Ⓜ Gamla Stan

Award-winning Leijontornet boasts the ruins of a 14th-century defence tower in its uberelegant dining room. But that's where the history ends, with culinary creations like squid with burnt leek or fried Mutzu apple with spruce-tree jelly and tar ice cream pushing the culinary envelope. The trendy **in-house bar** (www.leijonbaren.se; ⏱ 5pm-midnight Mon-Thu, 5pm-1am Fri & Sat) serves up fab midpriced fare and smooth DJ-spun tunes on Friday and Saturday.

# DRINK

### CHAIKHANA Teahouse

☎ 24 45 00; www.chaikhana.se; Svartmangatan 23; ⏱ 11am-7pm Mon-Fri, noon-6pm Sat & Sun; Ⓜ Gamla Stan

Haughtily tucked away from the camera-toting hordes shopping for trinkets along busy Västerlånggatan, this cosy tea salon is a hit with discerning locals. Join them for afternoon sessions of tea-sipping, pastry-nibbling and oh-so-subtle eavesdropping. If the strawberry and champagne mousse is on the menu, look no further.

### CHOKLADKOPPEN & KAFFEKOPPEN Cafe

☎ 20 31 70; Stortorget 18 & 20; ⏱ 9am-11pm Mon-Thu & Sun, to midnight Fri & Sat; Ⓜ Gamla Stan

If you haven't hung out at one of these cosy cafes, you just haven't 'done' Stockholm. The summer months see tables spilling out onto the square at these cafes,

NEIGHBOURHOODS

GAMLA STAN & RIDDARHOLMEN

which are set in a pair of fairy-tale 17th-century buildings on cobbled Stortorget. Bag a table, slip on some shades and eye up the passing talent.

### TORGET *Bar*
☎ 20 55 60; www.torgetbaren.com; Mälartorget 13; 🕑 4pm-1am Mon-Thu, 3pm-1am Fri, 1pm-1am Sat & Sun; Ⓜ Gamla Stan

For camp and Campari, it's hard to beat this sparkling gay bar – think rotating chandeliers, mock-baroque touches and different themed evenings, from live burlesque to handbag-swinging *schlager*. The sparkly crowd is a good source of info on upcoming underground parties, so grab yourself a champers and chat away, sweetie.

### WIRSTRÖMS PUB *Pub*
☎ 21 28 74; Stora Nygatan 13; 🕑 noon-1am Mon-Sat, 1pm-1am Sun; Ⓜ Gamla Stan

The charm of this expat-friendly pub is mostly to be found in its labyrinthine cellar, a warren of nooks and crannies that seems to go on forever. Grab a pint of Guinness and hide in a dark corner on a winter's day, or sit upstairs and socialise with chatty locals over the footie matches on the bigscreen TV.

Check out passers-by at cosy Chokladkoppen and Kaffekoppen (p47)

NEIGHBOURHOODS

GAMLA STAN & RIDDARHOLMEN

## WORTH THE TRIP

A 12-minute Tunnelbana trip south of Gamla Stan leads you to the extraordinarily beautiful cemetery of **Skogskyrkogården** ( ☎ 50 83 01 93; Sockenvägen 492, Enskede; admission free; ⏰ 24hr, visitors centre noon–5pm late May–Aug; Ⓜ Skogskyrkogården). This Unesco World Heritage–listed cemetery substitutes graveyard gloom for ethereal enchantment – picture soaring pines and soft streaming light. Designed by Sigurd Lewerentz and Gunnar Asplund (now buried here), the Woodland Cemetery is famed for its functionalist buildings, especially the crematorium, considered a highlight of 20th-century architecture and an example of Gunnar's ability to humanise functionalism.

Skogskyrkogården is also where Stockholm-native Greta Garbo (1905–90) finally got her wish to be left alone.

# PLAY

⭐ **LINO** *Gay & Lesbian*
www.linoclub.com; Södra Riddarholms-hamnen 19; admission Skr100; minimum age 23; ⏰ 10pm-3pm Sat; Ⓜ Gamla Stan

Lino is Stockholm's hottest gay party spot, packing a glitzy punch with its four bars, three dancefloors and mingle-friendly outdoor terrace for alfresco flirting. Disc-spinning talent includes *schlager*-master Edward af Sillén and club head honcho DJ Bernhard.

⭐ **STAMPEN** *Live Music*
☎ 20 57 93; www.stampen.se; Stora Nygatan 5; ⏰ 8pm-1am Mon-Thu, 8pm-2am Fri, 2-6pm & 8pm-2am Sat; Ⓜ Gamla Stan

This one-time pawn shop is better known as one of Stockholm's legendary music clubs, swinging to live blues and jazz every night. Past guests have included Swedish jazz great Monica Zetterlund, Woody Allen, and American blues legend Tino Gonzales, who rocked up unannounced one day, stepped up on stage and got grooving at Stampen's free Saturday Blues Jam (2pm to 6pm Saturday).

# >NORRMALM & VASASTADEN

Modernism rules in Norrmalm, Stockholm's restless commercial hub and home of the city's main train station, Centralstationen, and bus terminal Centralterminalen. Indiscriminately bulldozed in the 1960s, it's also where you'll find some of the capital's most controversial architectural icons, from the five-tower concoction of Hötorgscity to the severely modern Sergels Torg, a public square that is in fact round. Sergels Torg is home to another modernist lovechild, Kulturhuset – a huge glass shoe-box packed with theatres, art galleries and cafes.

While the epic National Museum continues the cultural theme, department store dame NK (Nordiska Kompaniet) heads the district's ripe retail mix.

To the north, Vasastaden is Stockholm's most densely populated residential district. Oozing a comfy lived-in vibe, its unfussed streets harbour funky galleries, off-beat shops, trendy cafes and the Blå Tornet, August Strindberg's former abode and now a museum dedicated to his life. It's also where you'll find some of Stockholm's finest eateries, from innovative Asian boltholes to the latest New Swedish darlings.

Centralstationen, Stockholm's main train station

NEIGHBOURHOODS

NORRMALM & VASASTADEN

# NORRMALM & VASASTADEN

Please see over for map

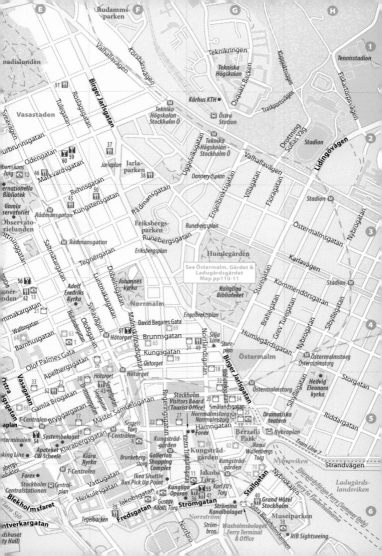

NEIGHBOURHOODS

NORRMALM & VASASTADEN

# SEE

### BIOGRAFEN SKANDIA

☎ 56 26 00 00; www.sf.se in Swedish; Drottninggatan 82; ⏰ check cinema schedules; Ⓜ Hötorget

LA has Mann's Chinese Theater, Melbourne has the Forum and Stockholm has this dreamy 1923 picture palace, designed by Gunnar Asplund and featuring a deep-blue vanishing ceiling and Pompeian rotunda in the lobby. Built inside the neo-Renaissance Warodell House (one of Stockholm's oldest apartment buildings), it's constantly threatening to close due to financial difficulties, so don't miss the chance to take a peek inside one afternoon or evening.

### BONNIERS KONSTHALL

☎ 736 42 48; www.bonnierskonsthall .se; Torsgatan 19; adult/under 18yr/concession Skr60/free/20; ⏰ noon-9pm Wed-Fri, to 5pm Sat & Sun; Ⓜ St Eriksplan; ♿

This ambitious gallery keeps culture fiends busy with a fresh dose of international contemporary art, as well as a reading room, a fab cafe and a busy diary of art seminars and artists-in-conversation sessions. The transparent clothes iron–shaped building is the work of Johan Celsing Arkitektkontor.

### BRÄNDSTRÖM & STENE

☎ 660 41 53; www.brandstromstene .com; Hudiksvallsgatan 6; admission free; ⏰ noon-6pm Thu & Fri, noon-4pm Sat & Sun; Ⓜ St Eriksplan; ♿

Tucked away in an anonymous industrial block, this is one of Stockholm's best private art galleries. It's famed for its intuitive sense for the next big thing, and past exhibitors have included Olafur Eliasson, Clay Ketter, Jan Håfström

## WORTH THE TRIP

Just north of Vasastaden awaits the regal refuge of **Hagaparken** ( Ⓜ Odenplan then bus 515 to Haga Norra), a sprawling 18th-century English-style park sprinkled with royal icons like Haga Slottet palace, eavesdropping **Ekotemplet** (Echo Temple; admission free; ⏰ 24hr) and **Slottsruinen**, a Versailles-inspired palace left incomplete after the assassination of King Gustav III in 1792.

Upstaging them all are the exotic **Koppartälten** ( ☎ 27 70 02; www.koppartalten.se in Swedish; ⏰ 10am-5pm May-Sep, 11am-4pm Oct-Apr), three magical copper tents created by set designer Louis-Jean Desprez in 1787. Originally a stable and barracks for Gustav III's personal guard, the central tent now houses the Haga Parkmuseum while the eastern tent boasts a slick cafe designed by Torbjörn Olsson.

and Jeppe Hein. A paint flick away is **Natalia Goldin Gallery** ( ☎ 650 21 35; www.nataliagoldin.com; Hudiksvallsgatan 8; admission free; 🕙 noon-6pm Wed-Fri, to 4pm Sat; M St Eriksplan; ♿ ), another pioneering art space best known for spotlighting hot new talent like photographer Martina Hoogland Ivanow and installation artist Sven Nilsson.

### ◐ DANSMUSEET
☎ 441 76 50; www.dansmuseet.se; Gustav Adolfs Torg 22-24; admission free, temporary exhibitions adult/under 19yr Skr70/free, Stockholm Card free; 🕙 11am-4pm Tue-Fri, noon-4pm Sat & Sun; M Kungsträdgården; ♿
The small yet sassy Dance Museum focuses on the intersections between dance, art and theatre. Collection highlights include vivid traditional dance masks from Africa, India and Tibet, avant-garde costumes from the Russian ballet, Chinese and Japanese theatre puppets and one of the world's finest collections of early-20th-century Ballets Russes costumes.

### ◐ GUSTAV VASA KYRKAN
☎ 736 03 35; Odenplan; admission free; 🕙 11am-6pm Mon-Thu, 11am-3pm Fri-Sun; M Odenplan
This saintly show-off flaunts a white Italian neo-baroque exterior and 60m-high cupola adorned

with dreamy New Testament frescoes by Vicke Andrén. Opened in 1906, its star attraction is Burchardt Precht's 18th-century marble altarpiece, considered Sweden's largest baroque sculpture. The creepy **columbarium crypt** ( ☎ 32 49 20; admission free; 🕙 11am-3pm Wed & Fri-Sun, 11am-6pm Tue & Thu) has places for around 35,000 burial urns; enter from the Västmannagatan side of the church.

### ◐ HALLWYLSKA MUSEET
☎ 402 30 99; www.hallwylskamuseet .se; Hamngatan 4; adult/under 19yr Skr60/free, Stockholm Card free; 🕙 11.45am-4pm Tue-Sun, 5.45-7pm Wed; M Östermalmstorg
Looking as if it's straight out of an Agatha Christie murder mystery, this kooky *fin de siècle* palace was once the home of cashed-up Count Walther von Hallwyl and his wife Wilhelmina, a notorious collector who took hoarding to new heights. The mansion's lavish rooms are packed with the fruits of her labour, from 16th-century tapestries and Flemish paintings to rare silver teapots, oriental guns, vintage toiletries and even her children's teeth. For in-depth voyeurism, join the one-hour guided tour (in English; Skr40; at 1pm Sunday, and at 1pm daily from late June to mid-August).

NEIGHBOURHOODS

NORRMALM & VASASTADEN

## JUDISKA MUSEET

☎ 31 01 43; www.judiska-museet.se; Hälsingegatan 2; adult/under 12yr/student/senior Skr60/free/20/40, Stockholm Card free; ⏱ noon-4pm Sun-Fri Mar-Oct, noon-4pm Sun-Thu, noon-2pm Fri Nov-Feb; Ⓜ Odenplan; ♿

Expanding Swedish history beyond Vasa and Vikings, this kosher little museum explores Swedish Jewry since 1774. Nifty pull-out display cabinets cover everything from the Holocaust and Raoul Wallenberg (a Swedish Oscar Schindler of sorts) to Torah silverware, ceremonial Passover items, wince-inducing circumcision knives, and a seven-branched candlestick looted from Jerusalem by the Romans in AD 70. The temporary exhibitions are often brilliant.

## KULTURHUSET

☎ 50 83 15 08; www.kulturhuset .stockholm.se; Sergels Torg 3; admission free, check website for theatre ticket prices; ⏱ 11am-9pm Tue-Fri, 11am-5pm Sat & Sun Sep-May, 11am-6pm Tue-Fri, 11am-4pm Sat & Sun Jun-Aug; Ⓜ T-Centralen; ♿

Culture House is the city's communal lounge room, packed with theatres (including Stockholms Stadsteater), free art galleries, a comic-book library, a chess-playing corner and even a crafts lounge where brooding teens can hang out, drink coffee and express themselves with art supplies and sewing machines. You'll find design shops and internet access in the basement and a brilliant cafe/restaurant on the 5th floor with monumental modernist views and a sunny summer terrace.

## MEDELHAVSMUSEET

☎ 51 95 53 80; Fredsgatan 2; admission Skr80, with Stockholm Card Skr40; ⏱ noon-8pm Tue-Fri, noon-5pm Sat & Sun, to 5pm Fri Jun-Aug; Ⓜ T-Centralen

Housed in an elegant Italianate building, this off-the-radar museum houses Egyptian, Greek, Cypriot, Roman and Etruscan artefacts in gorgeous rooms that enhance the appeal of the treasures. Those who love shiny things should visit the gold room, home to a 4th-century-BC olive wreath made of gold.

## NATIONAL MUSEUM

☎ 51 95 43 00; www.nationalmuseum .se; Södra Blasieholmshamnen; adult/child Skr100/free, Stockholm Card free; ⏱ 11am-8pm Tue & Thu, 11am-5pm Wed & Fri-Sun, to 5pm Thu Jun-Aug; Ⓜ Kungsträdgården; ♿

Sweden's largest art museum heaves with paintings, sculpture, drawings, decorative arts and graphics, from the Middle Ages through to the present. While there's no lack of continental bigwigs here, from Cézanne to Watteau, come for the Scandi stuff, which includes works by CG Pilo, Anders Zorn and Carl Larsson, whose commissioned staircase fresco, *Midwinter Sacrifice,* was originally rejected by the museum. Style buffs shouldn't miss the Design 19002000 exhibition.

### ☉ ST JAKOBS KYRKA

☎ 723 30 00; Jakobs torg 5; admission free; ☉ 11am-3pm Sep-May, 9am-6pm Jun-Aug; Ⓜ Kungsträdgården

Rising beside legendary opera house bistro Bakfickan (p65), this sorbet-hued church sits in the cosiest pocket of Norrmalm (picture bicycles, cobblestones and a continental vibe). Completed in 1643, the building features both Renaissance and Gothic architecture with a magnificent vaulted ceiling, an ornate pulpit (1828), high altarpiece (1937) and elaborate southern entrance.

### ☉ STADSBIBLIOTEKET

☎ 50 83 10 60; www.ssb.stockholm .se; Sveavägen 73; admission Skr50, tour Skr10; ☉ noon-4pm Tue-Sun Sep-May, 10am-4pm Tue-Sun Jun-Aug, tours in English 1.30pm Tue-Sun Jul; Ⓜ Rådmansgatan; &

Designed by Erik Gunnar Asplund in 1924, the Stockholm Public Library is one of Sweden's architectural masterpieces. A classic example of Nordic neoclassicism, its pièce de résistance is the breathtakingly beautiful cylindrical lending hall with its Technicolor panorama of books. Add artwork by Ivar Johnson in the vestibule and Nils Dardel in the children's library and you have yourself an unmissable Scandi treat.

Bobbing boats outside the National Museum

NEIGHBOURHOODS

NORRMALM & VASASTADEN

## UNDERGROUND ART

Stockholm's Tunnelbana (metro) has been coined the world's longest art exhibition, with over 140 artists contributing anything from sculpture, painting and etchings to engravings, mosaics and video installations at over 90 stations.

While the Blue Line boasts the best stuff overall, star stations across the network include cavernous Kungsträdgården (Map pp52–3, F5; waterfall, ferns and sculptures by Ulrik Samuelson), colourful Fridhemsplan (Map pp52–3, B5; Portuguese artist Dimas Macedo's sculptural tribute to the Swedish botanist Carl von Linne); Östermalmstorg (Map pp52–3, H4; reliefs on women's rights and the peace movement by Siri Derkert) and Universitetet (ceramic wall decorations by François Schein).

### STRINDBERGSMUSEET

☎ 411 53 54; www.strindbergsmuseet
.se; Drottninggatan 85; adult/under
19yr/concession Skr40/free/25; ⏲ noon-
4pm Tue-Sun, to 7pm Tue Mar-Sep, tours
in English (Skr10) 1.30pm Tue-Sun Jul;
Ⓜ Rådmansgatan

Set inside the Blå Tornet apartment where playwright and author August Strindberg spent his final four years, the Strindberg Museum lets you peep into his closet, scan his bookshelves and stumble across his desk, which still bears his pens, spectacles, theatrical program sheets and a copy of his *Ockulta Dagboken* (The Occult Diary, 1896–1908). The museum organises Strindberg-themed readings and seminars (occasionally in English; contact the museum for information). Those left longing for more should check out Strindberg's disturbingly dark paintings at the Nordiska Museet (p79).

### VIN & SPRITHISTORISKA MUSEET

☎ 744 70 70; www.vinosprithistoriska
.se; Dalagatan 100; adult/under 18yr/con-
cession Skr40/free/30, Stockholm Card
free; ⏲ 10am-7pm Tue, 10am-4pm Wed-
Fri, noon-4pm Sat & Sun; Ⓜ Odenplan

Looking at history through a snaps glass, this engrossing ode to grog explores the often turbulent relationship between Swedes and their beloved *brännvin* (akvavit) and *punsch* (a liqueur). Step inside a 19th-century wine merchant's distillery and happily sniff your way through 57 akvavit spices at the smelling organ. The wine bar hosts regular wine-tasting evenings (Skr350, book two weeks ahead), though you'll need a group of eight to knock back in English.

# SHOP

Norrmalm is the home to Stockholm's commercial heavyweights, including the department-store giants NK, Åhléns and the up-and-coming fashion hub PUB. Biblioteksgatan and Mäster Samuelsgatan are lined with fashionista magnets, while further north in Vasastaden, Upplandsgatan creaks with cute antiques.

### ☐ ACNE *Fashion*
☎ 611 64 11; www.acnejeans.com; Norrmalmstorg 2; ☽ 10am-7pm Mon-Fri, 10am-5pm Sat, noon-4pm Sun; Ⓜ Östermalmstorg

This is the flagship store for Stockholm's hottest label. Acne's threads, shoes and accessories for guys and girls cram the pages of *Vogue* and sell out in days in New York. The cult item here is the jeans, though we say good luck stopping there.

### ☐ ÅHLÉNS *Department Store*
☎ 676 60 00; www.ahlens.com; Klarabergsgatan 50; ☽ 10am-8pm Mon-Fri, 10am-7pm Sat, 11am-6pm Sun; Ⓜ T-Centralen

Looking better than ever after a revamp, this is the main branch of Sweden's best-known department store. All the standards are here from books, electronics and homewares to cosmetics and fashion, including the store's own very wearable label. Basement supermarket **Hemköp** ( ☽ 7am-9pm Mon-Fri, 10am-9pm Sat & Sun) sells ready-made vegetarian foods, while the

4th floor is home to a dreamy **day spa** ( ☎ 676 64 50; www.stockholmdayspa.se in Swedish).

### ☐ BEYOND RETRO *Vintage Clothing*
☎ 55 91 36 42; Mäster Samuelsgatan 56; ☽ 10am-8pm Mon-Fri, 10am-6pm Sat, 11am-5pm Sun; Ⓜ T-Centralen

The largest Stockholm location of this UK-based chain houses what seems like acres of retro threads. Quality varies a lot, so the best approach is to resign yourself to digging in and enjoying whatever surprises you find. Hats, party dresses and western shirts are your best bets. There's also a branch in Södermalm (Åsögatan 144).

### ☐ BOOKBINDERS *Stationery*
☎ 611 18 80; www.bookbindersdesign.com; Norrlandsgatan 20; ☽ 10am-6pm

### SHOP SWAP

In late 2006, Stockholm was hit by a case of retail Freaky Friday when fashion store Acne (left) swapped its premises and entire collection with London boutique Browns Focus. The shops, connected via a live video feed, swapped six staff from each store, who exchanged jobs and apartments for the 10-day event. The result? Acne-clad Londoners, Boudicca-clad Stockholmers, and the sweet smell of worldwide publicity.

NEIGHBOURHOODS

NORRMALM & VASASTADEN

More gorgeous blonde Swedes at NK department store (p62)

Mon-Fri, 10am-4pm Sat;
Ⓜ Östermalmstorg
Colour-code your life at this cult
stationery shop, famed for its stylish stationery in a range of tasty
tones. The hand-crafted, cloth-
covered notebooks will have you
itching to write, and there's a
range of matching diaries, photo
albums, cards and boxes to keep
your life in picture-perfect order.

### ▣ CHOKLADFABRIKEN
*Chocolate*
☎ 22 91 10; www.chokladfabriken
.com in Swedish; Regeringsgatan 58;

✎ 10am-6.30pm Mon-Fri, 10am-5pm
Sat; Ⓜ Hötorget
Get your cocoa fix at Stockholm's
finest chocolate shop. Owned by
one of Scandinavia's top choco-
latiers, its take-away box sets
make for seductive Stockholm
souvenirs. The main branch is in
Södermalm (p94).

### ▣ COW PARFYMERI *Cosmetics & Perfume*
☎ 611 15 04; www.cowparfymeri.se;
Mäster Samuelsgatan 9; ✎ 11am-6pm
Mon-Fri, 11am-4pm Sat; Ⓜ Östermalmstorg

Who said no one loves a cow? This cool cosmetics temple has no trouble pulling with its trend-setting range of perfumes, sticks and shades. Pick up rock-chic cosmetics from Urban Decay and Vincent Longo, or spray yourself silly with hard-to-find fragrances from Paris and New York. There's another outlet inside department store NK (p62).

### ☐ GUNNARSSONS TRÄFIGURER *Handicrafts*
☎ 21 67 17; u.gunnarsson@bostream.nu; Drottninggatan 77; ☽ 10am-6pm Mon-Fri, 11am-3pm Sat; Ⓜ Hötorget

In his Gepetto-style workshop, sci-fi fan and woodcarver Urban Gunnarsson cleverly carves statu-ettes (Skr950) of the famous and infamous. His sister Gisela paints each piece, which includes every US president since FD Roosevelt. Custom-made creations (fancy yourself in limewood?) take between two and four weeks and cost a significantly higher Skr4000.

### ☐ H&M *Fashion*
☎ 52 46 35 30; www.hm.com; Hamngatan 22; ☽ 10am-7pm Mon-Fri, 10am-6pm Sat, noon-5pm Sun; Ⓜ T-Centralen

Born and bred in Sweden, Hennes & Mauritz (H&M) is the fashion world's IKEA, selling well-made versions of each season's must-have fashions at cut-rate prices.

Guest designers have included Karl Lagerfeld. This branch is one of Stockholm's biggest and best.

### ☐ IRIS HANTVERK *Handicrafts*
☎ 21 47 26; Kungsgatan 55; ☽ 10am-6pm Mon-Fri, 10am-3pm Sat; Ⓜ Hötorget

Among other things, this shop sells handmade brushes tradition-ally crafted by visually impaired artisans. Made of birch and horsehair, they're as beautiful as they are functional, a principle that also applies to the rest of the handmade goods – linens, serving trays, soaps – available in the store.

### ☐ JUS *Fashion*
☎ 20 67 77; www.jus.se; Brunnsgatan 7; ☽ noon-6pm Tue-Fri, noon-4pm Sat; Ⓜ Hötorget

This grit-chic basement boutique stocks exquisite threads and a select choice of shoes and acces-sories for fashion-literate women and men. Expect Swedish labels like Rodeber and Pour, as well as There Goes The Neighborhood by Åsa Westlund, famous for her hand-painted clogs.

### ☐ MARIMEKKO *Textiles & Fashion*
☎ 440 32 75; www.marimekko.com; Norrmalmstorg 4; ☽ 10am-6.30pm Mon-Fri, 10am-5pm Sat; Ⓜ Östermalmstorg

Marimekko is to Finland what 10 Swedish Designers (p93) is to Sverige – its fresh retro patterns are the stuff of legend. And like its Swedish equivalent, the Finnish textile legend has plastered almost everything with its iconic prints, from towels, cups and coasters to notebooks, bags, napkins and clothes.

### MTWTFSS WEEKDAY Fashion

☎ 411 51 50; www.weekday.se; Olofsgatan 1; ⏰ 10am-8pm Mon-Fri, to 6pm Sat, noon-5pm Sun, basement to 6pm, to 4pm Sun Jul-Aug; Ⓜ Hötorget

Finding this once-hidden joint is a lot easier now that it has branches in two high-profile locations, one in Södermalm (on Götgatan) and one on Drottninggatan (at Kungsgatan), right around the corner from this, its original outpost. All the better for urban hipsters on a quest for street-smart, rock-star threads from the likes of Burfitt, Lois, April 77 and Swedish legend

Scandi style at NK department store

Cheap Monday, whose denim first hit the market at this very spot. Look for flyers announcing upcoming raves and indie gigs.

### NK Department Store

☎ 762 80 00; www.nk.se; Hamngatan 18-20; ⏰ 10am-7pm Mon-Fri, 10am-6pm Sat, noon-5pm Sun, noon-4pm Sun Jul–mid-Aug, basement closes 1hr later; Ⓜ T-Centralen

## RÖRSTRANDSGATAN

Running west from St Eriksplan Tunnelbana station, this little neighbourly strip (Map pp52–3, B3) is the perfect place for a low-key afternoon amble – the vibe is East Village meets Notting Hill. The street's flanks are lined with a homely mix of old-school grocery stores, small boutiques, buzzing bars and the odd bookshop. Bag fab Mexican chocolate at dessert bistro **Xoko** ( ☎ 31 84 87; www.xoko.se in Swedish; Rörstrandsgatan 15; ⏰ 7.30am-6.30pm Tue, 7.30am-11pm Wed-Fri, 9am-11pm Sat, 9am-6pm Sun) or get romantic over dinner or drinks at mod-Swedish **Paus Bar & Kök** ( ☎ 34 44 05; www.restaurangpaus.se in Swedish; Rörstrandsgatan 18; ⏰ 5pm-1am Mon-Sat, kitchen closes 11pm).

A Scandinavian Selfridges of sorts, this sleek retail palace boasts over 110 departments, amazing pastries in the basement food hall and a decent selection of English-language books. It's also infamous as the place where foreign minister Anna Lindh was murdered in 2003.

### NOSTALGIPALATSET
*Nostalgia*
☎ 34 00 61; www.nostalgipalatset.com; St Eriksgatan 101; ⏰ 11am-7pm Mon-Fri, 11am-3pm Sat; Ⓜ St Eriksplan
Need Diamanda Galas for a kinky cocktail session or a pinball machine for your Shoreditch loft? Chances are you'll find it at this must-see treasure trove, stacked high and wide with everything from rare vintage vinyl to 1950s Mexican film posters and retro toys in their original packaging.

### PLATINA *Jewellery*
☎ 30 02 80; www.platina.se; Odengatan 68; ⏰ 11am-6pm Mon-Fri, 11am-3pm Sat; Ⓜ Odenplan
Part gallery, part shop, forward-thinking Platina keeps things fresh with cutting-edge jewellery design from Sweden and beyond. Expect anything from Alice in Wonderland necklaces to pop-tastic hankies that 'drip' from your suit pocket lip.

**SHOPPING TIPS**
The best shops for:
> Cosmetics – Cow Parfymeri (p60)
> Cult designer furniture – Modernity (p116)
> Fashionista favourites – Mrs H (p115)
> Jewellery – Platina (left)
> Midcentury retro – Sivletto (p98)
> Sneakers – SneakersnStuff (p98)
> Young designer fashion – Tjallamalla (p99)
> Obscure collectables – Nostalgipalatset (left)

### RECORD HUNTER *Music*
☎ 32 20 23; www.recordhunter.se in Swedish; St Eriksgatan 70; ⏰ 11am-7pm Mon-Fri, 11am-5pm Sat, noon-4pm Sun; Ⓜ St Eriksplan
It's places like this that make St Eriksgatan one of Stockholm's best streets for…well, record hunting. It has a heaving sale rack in the basement, a decent selection of dirt-cheap retro vinyl, secondhand DVDs and a kids' music section. Best of all, you can pick up tickets to major music gigs.

### WESC *Fashion*
☎ 21 25 15; www.wesc.com; Kungs-gatan 66; ⏰ 11am-6pm Mon-Fri, 10am-4pm Sat; Ⓜ Hötorget
This street-smart label got started by dressing up underground artists and musos. In less than a

NEIGHBOURHOODS

NORRMALM & VASASTADEN

## EMPIRE IKEA

Forget ABBA and Volvos – when it comes to Swedish icons, IKEA beats the lot. In 2007, 253 patriotically toned showrooms fringed freeways and ring-roads in 24 countries. The annual store catalogue is the world's most printed work (over 200 million copies in 2008) and it's estimated that one in 10 Europeans are conceived in an IKEA bed.

Despite the fact it's now a Dutch-registered company, Stockholm boasts the biggest **IKEA store** ( ☎ 020 43 90 50; www.ikea.se; Kungens Kurva, Skärholmen; ⏰ 10am-8pm Mon-Fri, 10am-6pm Sat & Sun; 🚌 173, 707, 710, 748).

For a glimpse (we know you want to), catch the free shuttle bus departing outside the southeast entrance to the Gallerian shopping centre on Regeringsgatan (Map pp52–3, F5) every hour on the hour from 10am to 7pm Monday to Friday.

decade, it's become one of Sweden's fashion big guns, opening up stores from Seoul to Beverly Hills (actor Jason Lee is a fan). The look is indie-meets-skater cool, with all bases covered, from lusty denim to pimp-a-licious silk hoods for trendy dudes and sistas.

###  WHYRED *Fashion*
☎ 660 01 70; www.whyred.se; Mäster Samuelsgatan 5; ⏰ 10am-7pm Mon-Fri, 10am-5pm Sat, noon-4pm Sun; Ⓜ Östermalmstorg
Fashion-literate Swedes can't get enough of designer Roland Hjort's understated clothes – think preppy-college meets street-smart. The guys' sweaters are particularly fine and the women's shoes are irresistible.

## 🍴 EAT
Going hungry is not an option on these downtown streets. From

budget bites to super-fine feasting, there's a battered bench and linen-lined table to satisfy every whim. Pig out at an ethnic market, dig into Ethiopian *mesobs* or toast the high life in an opera-house dining room. For top-notch Asian grub, head straight to Luntmakargatan; it's Stockholm's quasi-Chinatown sans the lanterns and dragon kitsch.

### 🍴 ABYSSINIA *Ethiopian* €€
☎ 33 08 40; www.abyssinia.se in Swedish; Vanadisvägen 20; ⏰ 11am-11pm Mon-Fri, 2-11pm Sat; Ⓜ Odenplan; Ⓥ
Forget what your mother said and eat with yours hands at this down-to-earth gem, which serves up authentic, award-winning Ethiopian grub in Technicolor *mesobs* (traditional woven baskets). The multi-flavoured Abyssinia Special is unmissable (carnivorous, vegetarian or vegan option), as is the heavenly Ethio-

pian coffee – made to a secret recipe you'll never know, no matter how sweetly you ask.

### 🍴 BAKFICKAN Swedish €€

☎ 676 58 09; www.operakallaren.se; Karl XII's Torg; ⏲ 11.30am-11.30pm Mon-Fri, noon-11.30pm Sat; Ⓜ Kungsträdgården

Set in the opera house and appropriately crammed with opera photographs and deco-style lampshades, this buzzing counter restaurant is famed for its savvy old-school waiters and top-notch *husmanskost* (traditional Swedish fare); Bakfickan shares a kitchen with Operakällaren (p69). A great place for solo supping, it's best late at night, when you're bound to stumble across a bitching soprano.

### 🍴 CAFFÉ NERO Cafe €

☎ 22 19 35; Roslagsgatan 4; ⏲ 7.30am-10pm Mon-Sat, 10am-5pm Sun; Ⓜ Rådmansgatan

Delectable Italian waiters and a brutally chic concrete interior give Caffé Nero the thumbs up with Vasastaden hipsters. They all flock here for mighty *caffé*, grappa shots, Italian home-cooking (the veal meatballs are sublime) and a creamy tiramisu that's worth the damage.

### 🍴 ESPERANTO Fusion €€€

☎ 696 23 23; www.esperantorestaurant .se in Swedish; Kungstensgatan 2; ⏲ lunch 11.30am-6pm Mon-Fri, dinner 6pm-1am Tue-Sat; Ⓜ Rådmansgatan

Hailed as the new Bon Lloc (a now-defunct restaurant renowned for its avant-garde cooking), award-winning Esperanto offers a five- or seven-course menu only (Skr855/995). While the servings are notoriously petite, creations like duck challandaise with blood orange curd and breadcréme served with liquorice and tangerine will leave you gratified. A culinary event; book weeks in advance.

### WORTH THE TRIP

For the ultimate dining indulgence, book a table at one of only two Michelin two-star restaurants in Sweden, **Edsbacka Krog** ( ☎ 96 33 00; www.edsbackakrog.se; Sollentunavägen 220, Sollentuna; ⏲ 5.30pm-midnight Mon-Fri, 2pm-midnight Sat; J-train to Sollentuna Centrum, then 🚌 525, 527, 607). Set snugly in an inn dating back to 1626 and headed by Christer Lingström (Sweden's culinary ambassador), its seasonal Swedish-French menu will send shivers up your spine – the things Lingström does to salmon, scallops, lobster, lamb and rabbit are criminally good.

Across the street, **Edsbacka Bistro** ( ☎ 631 00 34; Sollentunavägen 223; ⏲ 5.30pm-midnight Tue-Sat) serves up simpler, cheaper grub with the same Lingström finesse.

**Daniel Lampinen**
*Author, Temporary Stockholmer blog*
*(temporarystockholmer.blogspot.com)*

**Why Stockholm?** I've been a Stockholmer since 1999, when I moved here from a medium-sized town in the far north. I wanted the feeling of being close to the centre of things. At first I lived in different concrete ghettos, the kind with (almost) immigrants only, which I liked a lot more than the notion of living in suburbs that weren't special in any way. In 2007 I started renting a wooden cabin (5x2m) in the extreme east of the archipelago. In the woods. By the water. So now I've had the best of both worlds within Stockholm. **Best thing about Stockholm?** That you are close to the most interesting people Sweden has to offer. The skyline view from Katarinavägen is underrated, and when I bring visitors there I say that I'm grateful for having that in my every-day life. **Worst?** The fast-food prices. I just want to eat something. My rule of never spending more than Skr60 for a full meal has pretty much left me with Jerusalem Kebab (p101). But at least Sweden has good falafel. **Oddest?** In the subway Stockholmers have become experts at looking at nothing in the air, between two heads, instead of looking at the person sitting right across, because of how the seats come in groups of four.

## 🍴 FREDSGATAN 12
*New Swedish*   €€€

☎ 24 80 52; www.fredsgatan12.com; Fredsgatan 12; 🕙 11.30am-2pm & 5pm-1am Mon-Fri, 5pm-1am Sat; M T-Centralen

Chef Melker Andersson's award-winning baby, Fredsgatan 12 (F12) is another culinary adventure – think squid and sea buckthorn with oyster emulsion, shredded black bread and cucumber, veal tenderloin with lobster and tarragon, and pear fudge with ginger and cardamom. It's all served in one of the city's slinkiest dining spaces, so book ahead. Alternatively, settle for rare Danish beers at the bar or summertime mojitos on the hugely popular outdoor *terrasen* (terrace).

## 🍴 GRANDS VERANDA
*Swedish*   €€€

☎ 679 35 86; Grand Hôtel Stockholm, Södra Blasieholmshamnen 8; 🕙 7am-11pm; M Kungsträdgården

Located inside the venerable Grand Hôtel, the **smörgåsbord** (🕙 1-4pm & 6-10pm Sat & Sun Feb, 6-10pm Mon-Fri, 1-4pm & 6-10pm Sat & Sun Mar, Apr & Sep-Nov, noon-3pm & 6-10pm Mon-Fri, 1-4pm & 6-10pm Sat & Sun May-Aug, Christmas buffet Dec) here is Stockholm's best. Get in early for a window seat and feast away on old-school favourites like *gravad-lax* (cured salmon) with a moreish

mustard sauce. The hotel's newest dining spot, Restaurant Mathias Dahlgren, named after its Bocuse d'Or-winning chef, has garnered a second Michelin star as well as top marks for comfort and service.

## 🍴 HAGA RESTAURANG & DELIKATESSER
*Italian*   €€€

☎ 31 96 95; www.hagadeli.com in Swedish; Hagagatan 18; 🕙 11am-11pm Mon-Wed, 11am-midnight Thu-Sat, 5-10pm Sun; M Odenplan

Deli-style wall tiles, flickering candlelight and a smattering of old Italian film posters set the tone for classic Italian favourites with a naughty Nordic twist. While the pizzas are fine, consider yourself blessed if the stuffed squid is on the menu.

## 🍴 HATTORI SUSHI DEVIL
*Sushi*   €€

☎ 22 44 00; Tegnérgatan 43; 🕙 11am-9pm Mon-Fri, 1-9pm Sat; M Rådmansgatan

Busier than a Shinjuku subway stop, this slick little sushi bar rolls out sushi so good it could make a sumo wrestler weep. The complimentary miso soup is top-notch, the fish is filthy-fresh and the artful *nigiri* (sushi rice with fish on top) is well worth the lunchtime queues.

## AT THE SMÖRGÅSBORD

A traditional hit in the lead-up to Christmas, Sweden's lip-smacking smörgåsbord or *julbord* (Christmas table) is a soul-satisfying, waist-expanding journey through old-school Scandi flavours. For successful smörgåsbord navigation, start with the herring dishes, accompanied by boiled potatoes and crispbread, and best washed down with a cool aquavit. Done, move on to the more substantial fare – *gravadlax* (cured salmon), lemon-drizzled eel, smoked salmon, fried shortribs, meatballs with lingonberries, stockfish and *Janssons frestelse* (Jansson's Temptation), a dangerously rich potato-and-onion casserole loaded with double cream and anchovies. Use a clean dish each time, and never overload your plate – in the land of *lagom* (the Swedish concept of 'everything in moderation'), shameless excess is just oh-so-nej. For classic smörgåsbord all year long, pull up a chair at the trad-fab Grands Veranda (p67).

### 🍴 HÖTORGSHALLEN *Market* €
www.hotorgshallen.se in Swedish; Hötorget; 🕐 10am-6pm Mon-Fri, 10am-3pm Sat Jun & Jul, 10am-6pm Mon-Thu, 10am-6.30pm Fri, 10am-4pm Sat Aug-May; Ⓜ Hötorget

Located in the basement below Filmstaden cinema, this electric food market serves up the best of multicultural Stockholm, from garlic souvlakis to hearty delicate prosciutto. Bag some Swedish berries, bite into baklava or bag a table at galley-themed Kaysas Fiskrestaurang for huge bowls of fish stew with mussels, aioli and a free small beer (Skr80).

### 🍴 KONDITORI RITORNO *Cafe* €
☎ 32 01 06; Odengatan 80-82; 🕐 7am-10pm Mon-Thu, 7am-8pm Fri, 8am-6pm Sat, 10am-6pm Sun; Ⓜ Odenplan

The cosy back room at this un-presumptuous cafe looks like the lobby of an antique movie house fallen on hard times. A hit with writers, students and pensioners, its worn leather couches and miniature jukeboxes at every table make it a perfect pitstop for old-school shrimp sandwiches and heavenly semla buns.

### 🍴 LAO WAI
*Chinese Vegetarian* €€€
☎ 673 78 00; www.laowai.se; Luntmakargatan 74; 🕐 lunch 11am-2pm Mon-Fri, dinner 5-9pm Tue-Sat; Ⓜ Rådmansgatan; Ⓥ

You can forget about soggy chick-pea mush at Lao Wai, arguably the best vegetarian joint in town. The slick Chinese repertoire includes a superb gluten-free and vegan Ma Po Dou Fu (spicy Sichuan vegetarian 'meat' dressed in chilli bean sauce, ginger, garlic and spring onion) and the equally irresistible Hong Shao Su Rou (soy 'meat', champignons, Chinese broccoli, cloud ears and sweet pepper braised in a five-spice soy sauce).

## 🍴 MOONCAKE
*Asian Fusion* €€€
☎ 16 99 28; www.mooncake.se; **Luntmakargatan 95;** ⏱ 11am-2.30pm Mon-Fri, 5-11pm Mon-Sat; Ⓜ **Rådmansgatan**

Stick a Hong Kong chef behind a wok and watch the crowds roll in. The inventive menu at this elegant Eastern hotspot includes crispy rösti crab and prawn cakes (Skr95) and the delicate drunken Szechuan duck with tamarind-chilli glaze (Skr237). It's all sublime and complemented by discreet, near-perfect service.

## 🍴 OPERAKÄLLAREN
*French* €€€
☎ 676 58 01; www.operakallaren .se; Karl XII's Torg; ⏱ 6-10pm Tue-Sat; Ⓜ **Kungsträdgården**

If you plan on proposing, this is the place to do it. Inside Stockholm's 19th-century opera house, decadent chandeliers, golden mirrors and exquisitely carved ceilings are elegantly paired with classic French fare fused with subtle contemporary twists – think chicken stuffed with truffle and served with liver sauce, venison drizzled in blackcurrant jus and Russian tea sorbet with a refreshing orange mousse. Gents, wear a suit and tie, and book a table at least two weeks ahead.

Grab some grub at Hötorgshallen

### 🍴 PONTUS!
*French-Swedish*                    €€€

☎ 54 52 73 00; Brunnsgatan 1;
🕙 11.30am-2pm Mon-Fri, 5-11pm Mon-Sat; Ⓜ Östermalmstorg

Down Thai mojitos and super sushi at the trendy bar, or head one floor down for luxe dining at chi-chi circular booths. French and Swedish cooking fill out a menu with three themes: harvest, season, and caught. Chefs transform fair-trade, organic and local produce into the likes of boiled lobster with smoked Swedish duck, brioche and preserved plum. DJs spin records on weekends.

### 🍴 REPUBLIK *French Fusion* €€€

☎ 54 59 05 50; www.restaurant-republik.com; Tulegatan 17; 🕙 11am-3pm Mon, 11am-midnight Tue-Thu, 11am-1am Fri, 5pm-1am Sat; Ⓜ Rådmansgatan

Republik's trés urbane bar was voted Stockholm's best in 2006 (try a Gasper cocktail and you'll see why), yet the ultimate indulgence here is the restaurant, where the vibe is suave, the staff clued-up and the French-influenced food scandalously good (the seared scallops with truffle risoni, jamón Serrano, romanesco and fennel dill will leave you with a post-dinner glow).

### 🍴 SIBIRIENS SOPPKÖK *Soup* €

☎ 15 00 14; www.sibirienssoppkok.com in Swedish; Roslagsgatan 25;

🕙 10am-10pm Mon-Fri, noon-10pm Sat; Ⓜ Tekniska Högskolan

Sibiriens makes soup sexy; a table at this intimate bolthole is a prized possession, so book ahead or turn up before 11am or between 3pm and 5pm. The star attraction is the house fish soup of lobster, shrimps, salmon, cream and cognac. Luxe liquids aside, the changing daily menu also brims with tapas, pasta and Med-leaning wines.

### 🍴 VETEKATTEN *Cafe*          €

☎ 20 84 05; www.vetekatten.se in Swedish; Kungsgatan 55; 🕙 7.30am-8pm Mon-Fri, 9am-5pm Sat, noon-5pm Sun; Ⓜ Hötorget

Vintage Vetekatten keeps the treadmills running with its can't-stop-at-one Swedish treats, from vanilla and almond buns to fabulously fluffy *kanelbulle* (cinnamon buns). Packed with cute small rooms, it's the perfect spot for discreet gluttons.

# 🍸 DRINK

In Norrmalm, spangly bars like Café Opera keep the vibe chic and cliquey. For laid-back cool, head to much-loved Vasastaden favourites like the fabulously flirty Storstad and the quasi-kink of Olssons.

### 🍸 ABSOLUT ICEBAR *Bar*

☎ 50 56 31 24; www.nordichotels.se; inside the Nordic Sea Hotel, Vasaplan 4;

admission Skr180; ⏱ drop-in 9.45pm-
1am Fri & Sat, reservations recommended
all other times; Ⓜ T-Centralen
Okay, it's touristy. But you're
intrigued, admit it: a bar built
entirely out of ice, where you drink
from glasses carved of ice at tables
made of ice. The admission price
gets you warm booties, mittens, a
parka and one drink. Refill drinks
costs Skr85.

### Ⓨ CAFÉ OPERA
*Restaurant, Bar & Nightclub*
☎ 676 58 07; Operahuset, Karl XII's
Torg; admission nightclub after 10pm
Skr150; ⏱ 5pm-3am Tue-Sat, 7am-3am
Sun; Ⓜ Kungsträdgården
Wannabe playboys and their
glitzy girlfriends need a suitably
excessive place to schmooze,
preferably one with bulbous
chandeliers, haughty ceiling
frescoes and a spangly party
vibe. This is it, darlings. In sharp
contrast, the adjoining Veranden
bar is a crisp white creation by
architect trio Claesson Koivisto
Rune and a favourite hangout for
bartenders, meaning a mediocre martini is strictly out of the
question.

### Ⓨ GRILL *Restaurant & Bar*
☎ 31 45 30; www.grill.se; Drottninggatan 89; ⏱ bar 5pm-1am Mon-Thu
& Sat, 4pm-1am Fri, 5-11pm Sun;
Ⓜ Rådmansgatan

If you like to stay in and drink at
home, then head out to Grill. This
iconic resto-bar, owned by the
equally iconic chef Melker Andersson, is set in a furniture showroom,
so you can choose a setting and
play house with your pals (as long
as you don't mind the odd pink
flamingo and gold lamé drape á la
Versace).

### Ⓨ KGB *Restaurant & Bar*
☎ 20 91 55; www.kgb-bar.com;
Malmskillnadsgatan 45; ⏱ 4pm-2am
Mon-Sat; Ⓜ Hötorget
Skip the hit-and-miss menu at this
ode to Red Russia (think Lenin
statue, communist banners and a
Stalin-wannabe cloakroom attend-
ant) and head straight down to
the gritty bunker-style bar. Here,
laid-back indie types get happy on
vodka, DJ tunes and fortnightly
Friday bands.

### Ⓨ MUSSLAN *Seafood Bar*
☎ 34 64 10; www.musslan.se; Dalagatan 46; ⏱ 6pm-1am Tue-Wed, to 2am
Thu-Sat; Ⓜ Odenplan
If you like a little French hip hop
with your mussels, this tiny dark
den is for you. One of Stockholm's
best spots for seafood (try a bowl
of whelks from Brittany), it's also a
good bet for lounging to DJ-spun
indie pop, deep house and reggae
under the stars (they're painted on
the ceiling).

### ▼ OLSSONS *Video Bar*

☎ 673 38 00; www.olssonsvideo.se in Swedish; Odengatan 41; ⏱ 9pm-3am Wed, Thu & Sat, 6pm-3pm Fri; Ⓜ Rådmansgatan

While the retro neon signage, dark tinted mirrors, dancing pole and cucumber cocktail might allude to a kinky disposition, this Vasastaden favourite was actually once a shoe shop. The 'video' in 'video bar' refers to the Studio 54–style films projected onto a screen, which is easily upstaged by the hip young crowd, super-cool tunes (from retro to electro) and mighty red mojitos. Head in before 10pm or be prepared to queue.

### ▼ STORSTAD *Restaurant & Bar*

☎ 673 38 00; www.storstad.se in Swedish; Odengatan 41; ⏱ 5pm-1am Mon-Thu, 4pm-3am Fri & Sat; Ⓜ Rådmansgatan

Years later, the queues are still going long and strong at this slinky resto-bar. Could it be the fab French grub, killer cocktails or smooth sexy tunes? Personally, we think it's the infamously flirty crowd. Once again, head in early or join the queue.

### ▼ TENNSTOPET
*Pub & Restaurant*

☎ 32 25 18; www.tennstopet.se in Swedish; Dalagatan 50; ⏱ 4pm-1am Mon-Fri, 1pm-1am Sat & Sun; Ⓜ Odenplan

Had there been a Swedish version of *Cheers*, it would've been filmed here. Oil paintings, gilded mirrors and winter candlelight set the scene for a loveable cast of wizened regulars, corner-seat scribes and melancholy dames. Watch the show with a soothing *öl* (beer) and a serve of soulful *husmanskost*.

##  PLAY

### BERNS SALONGER *Restaurant, Bar, Live Music, Nightclub*

☎ 56 63 20 00; www.berns.se; Berzelii Park; ⏱ to 3am; Ⓜ Kungsträdgården

---

## FROM SILVER SCREEN TO URBAN SEAMS

That the exterior of trendy concept store **Urban Outfitters** (Biblioteksgatan 5) has a certain star quality is no coincidence. The building used to house the Röda Kvarn (Moulin Rouge), a gorgeous vintage picture palace. While the projectors have gone, the heritage features remain, from the decadent chandeliers to the beautiful hardwood details. Where film buffs once sat, House of Holland T-shirts sit beside Dita Von Teese art books and Bad Boyfriend Voodoo Dolls. Fitting rooms line the grand old stage behind a kitschy mock-chateau facade, and the upstairs foyers now premiere the work of new Stockholm artists. A case of clever conservation or consumerist degradation? You be the judge.

While the drop-dead gorgeous ballroom here hosts some brilliant live-music gigs, Berns' hottest drawcard is the intimate basement bar/club, Berns 2.35:1, open 9pm to 4am Wednesday to Saturday. It's packed with hip creative types, top-notch DJs and art projections. Entry is via the Berns Hotel around the corner (Näckströmsgatan 8). Entry is by invitation only; contact Berns to be put on the guest list.

### ⭐ CENTRALBADET *Spa*
☎ 24 24 02; www.centralbadet.se; **Drottninggatan 88; adult/concession Skr130/70, Skr180 after 3pm Fri & Sat;** ⏰ **6am-8pm Mon-Fri, 8am-8pm Sat, 8am-5pm Sun, closed Sun Jul;** Ⓜ **Hötorget**
Sturebadet's (p125) humbler rival, this loveable art nouveau spa centre is the perfect spot for a thermal dip, soak or workout. Go early in the day to avoid the masses and book massage treatments a week in advance. The hire of swimming kit, robes and towels means an impromptu dip is never out of the question.

### ⭐ DANSENS HUS
*Contemporary Dance*
☎ 50 89 90 90; www.dansenshus.se; **Barnhusgatan 12-14; tickets Skr160-300;** ⏰ **box office 2-6pm Mon-Fri, 2-7pm Sat during performances;** Ⓜ **Hötorget**

The stomping ground of Mats Ek's Cullberg Ballet is a must for contemporary dance fans. The packed program showcases anything from the Royal Swedish Ballet's spin-off troupe Stockholm 59°N to international big guns like Les Ballets C de la B and hot UK choreographer Hofesh Shechter.

### ⭐ GLENN MILLER CAFÉ
*Live Music*
☎ 10 03 22; **Brunnsgatan 21A;** ⏰ **5pm-1am Mon-Thu, to 2am Fri & Sat;** Ⓜ **Hötorget**
Loaded with character, and characters, this jazz and blues bar has a lively regular crowd and a stellar line-up of musical performers. It's small, so prepare to get cosy. The menu is as unpretentious as the venue, with Swedish homestyle dishes and French classics.

### ⭐ JAZZCLUB FASCHING
*Jazz Club*
☎ 53 48 29 60; www.fasching.se in **Swedish; Kungsgatan 63; tickets Skr50-225;** ⏰ **7pm-1am Mon-Thu, 7pm-4am Fri & Sat;** Ⓜ **T-Centralen**
Fasching turns Swedish sobriety on its head with kick-ass jazz, swing and tango jams from local and international cool cats. Late Friday nights, DJs spin everything from reggae to latin to hip hop at various club nights (Skr100; from midnight to 4am), while Saturday

Strindbergsmuseet (p58)

club night Soul (Skr100; from midnight to 4am) is a funkalicious mix of retro R&B, soul jazz, disco and funk.

### ☆ KONSERTHUSET Concert Hall
☎ 50 66 77 88; www.konserthuset .se; Hötorget; tickets Skr65-400; ⊗ box office 11am-6pm Mon-Fri, 11am-3pm Sat; Ⓜ Hötorget

Designed by Ivar Tengbom in 1926 and decked out in Carl Milles sculptures, Stockholm's Concert Hall is home to the brilliant Royal Stockholm Philharmonic Orchestra. Pick up a schedule at the office inside Konserthuset (en-

trance on Kungsgatan) or check the website.

### ☆ KUNGSANS ISBANA
Outdoor Ice Skating
☎ 55 51 00 90; Kungsträdgården; skate hire adult/child per hr Skr40/20; ⊗ 9am-6pm Mon, Thu & Fri, 9am-9pm Tue & Wed, 10am-6pm Sat & Sun Nov-early Mar, cashier closes 1hr before closing; Ⓜ Kungsträdgården

Kitsch and endearing in equal measure, this popular winter ice rink in Kungsträdgården is the perfect antidote to sightseeing overload. Surrounded by icons like St Jakobs Kyrka and the omnipresent NK sign, it's a great place to exercise, exorcise, crash into a hottie or simply sing along to A-ha's Take On Me.

### ☆ NALEN
Live Music
☎ 453 34 00; www.nalen.com in Swedish; Regeringsgatan 74; tickets free-Skr360; ⊗ restaurant 11.30am-11pm Mon-Fri, 5-11pm Sat, downstairs bar 6pm-2am Fri & Sat; Ⓜ Hötorget

First a dancehall, then a church, plush-looking Nalen is back to its old tricks, pumping out infectious live gigs from jazz and indie soul to sing-song synths. There are three halls, open when bands are playing, so scan the website for upcoming gigs. The downstairs bar is tiny and crowded.

## ⭐ NYBROKAJEN 11
*Chamber & World Music*

☎ 407 17 00; www.nybrokajen11
.rikskonserter.se; Nybrokajen 11; tickets
Skr60-200; ⌚ box office noon-5pm
Mon-Fri & 2hr before concerts, closed
mid-Jun–Aug; Ⓜ Kungsträdgården
The former home of the Royal
Academy of Music now accommo-
dates the Rikskonserter (Swedish
Concert Institute). The graceful
main hall boasts killer acous-
tics and hosts mostly local and
international chamber music.
The smaller adjoining **Stallet**, a converted stable, is home to Swedish
folk and world music.

## ⭐ STRINDBERGS
INTIMATEATER *Theatre*

☎ 20 08 43; www.strindbergsintima
teater.se in Swedish; Barnhusgatan 20;
tickets Skr50-200; ⌚ box office noon-
2pm Tue-Fri; Ⓜ Hötorget

Established by the great scribe
himself, this small stage has seen
many a Strindberg premiere,
including *The Ghost Sonata*, *Miss
Julie* and *Svanevit*. These days, the
repertoire has broadened, with
collaborative partners including Dramaten (Royal Dramatic
Theatre) and the New York Actors
Studio. Most productions are in
Swedish.

## ⭐ TRANAN
*Restaurant, Bar, Music*

☎ 30 07 65; www.tranan.se; Karl-
bergsvägen 14; ⌚ 7pm-1am daily;
Ⓜ Odenplan
We dare you to find a local who
doesn't adore this basement bar.
Right next to the excellent same-
name restaurant, it's a chilled-out
spot for DJ-spun hip hop and
house, live indie bands and laid-
back suits and hipster crowds.

# >DJURGÅRDEN & SKEPPSHOLMEN

Whether you arrive on vintage tram 9 or the ferry from Slussen, dreamy Djurgården (p17) is bound to leave you smitten with its fairy-tale woods and bird-rich marshes. Acquired by King Karl Knutsson in 1452, this former royal hunting ground also played host to the Stockholm Expo in 1897. Six years earlier on the island, Artur Hazelius had set up Skansen, the world's first alfresco museum and still one of Stockholm's unmissable sights. Not that Djurgården has any shortage of must-see magnets, from the colossal calamity of the *Vasa* to classic Scandi art at Thielska Galleriet and Prins Eugens Waldemarsudde.

To the west, the smaller island of Skeppsholmen proves the adage that good things come in small packages. This one-time shipbuilding hub boasts an impressive museum line-up, including the mighty Moderna Museet, Arkitekturmuseet, Fotografins Hus and design hub Svensk Form. It also sets the scene for romantic twilight ambling, from turreted vistas to the north to Slussen's Hong Kong neon to the east.

# DJURGÅRDEN & SKEPPSHOLMEN

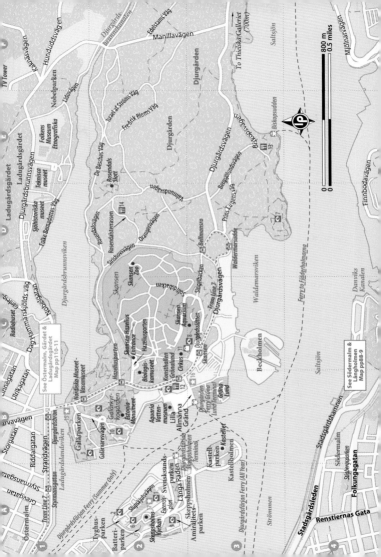

#  SEE

## ARKITEKTURMUSEET

☎ 58 72 70 00; www.arkitekturmuseet
.se; Exercisplan 4; adult/under 18yr
Skr50/free, Stockholm Card free, Fri free;
🕓 10am-8pm Tue, 10am-6pm Wed-Sun;
🚌 65

Attached to the Moderna Museet and housed in an ex-military drill hall, the Museum of Architecture's permanent exhibition covers 1000 years of Swedish architecture (from cabins to the contemporary) and boasts an archive of 2.5 million documents, photographs, plans, drawings and models. There's a seasonal program of temporary exhibitions, and the museum hosts occasional seminars on everything from urban planning to future design.

## FOTOGRAFINS HUS

☎ 611 69 69; www.fotografinshus.se;
Slupskjulsvägen 26A; admission Skr50;
🕓 noon-7pm Tue & Wed, noon-5pm
Thu-Sun; 🚌 65

Currently under renovation, but set to reopen by press time, this is one of Stockholm's best sites for photographic art. Decked out in furniture designed by Konstfack graduates, its six annual exhibitions showcase local and international talent, with past exhibitors including Hasselblad prize-winner David Goldblatt, Susan Heiselas and J H Engström,

Sweden's Wolfgang Tillmans. You'll find their signatures on the foyer wall, behind which awaits a cosy little cafe.

## JUNIBACKEN

☎ 58 72 30 00; www.junibacken.se;
Galärparken; adult/children & seniors
Skr125/110, Stockholm Card free;
🕓 10am-5pm Tue-Sun Sep-May, 10am-
5pm daily Jun & Aug, 9am-6pm daily Jul;
🚌 47; 🚊 7; ♿

A must for children (and the child within), this whimsical theme park recreates scenes from Astrid Lindgren's children's books. Catch the flying Story Train over Stockholm, shrink to the size of a sugar cube and end up at Villekulla cottage where kids can shout, squeal and dress up like Pippi Longstocking. There's a cafe and a well-stocked children's bookshop. The best time to visit is midweek, when the queues won't test your smile.

## LILJEVALCHS KONSTHALL

☎ 50 83 13 30; www.liljevalchs
.com; Djurgårdsvägen 60; adult/under
18yr/concession Skr70/free/50, Stockholm Card free; 🕓 11am-5pm Wed &
Fri-Sun, to 8pm Tue & Thu; 🚌 47; 🚊 7

If you're in town February to mid-March, the Vårsalongen Art Show held here is a fun place to shop for high art and kitsch from both new and established Swedish artists. Otherwise, come for

## THE STORYBOOK SECRETARY

When Astrid Lindgren's daughter Karin fell ill in 1941, she asked her mother for a story. Lindgren, then a Stockholm secretary, made one up about a mischievous freckled girl called Pippi Longstocking. The tale quickly became a hit with Karin and her friends.

While recovering from a sprained ankle in 1944, Lindgren finally put her tale to paper and sent it to a publisher. Rejected but undefeated, she sent a second story to another publisher and scooped up second prize in a girls' story competition. The following year, a revamped Pippi manuscript grabbed top honours in another competition, while her story 'Bill Bergson Master Detective' shared first prize in 1946.

When the Queen of the Bedtime Story died in 2002, her impressive output of work included plays, songs and books translated into over 50 languages.

the neoclassical architecture, Carl Milles statues by the entrance and top-notch temporary exhibitions of modern art, which range from video, photography and sculpture to painting, drawing and etching.

### MODERNA MUSEET

☎ 51 95 52 00; www.modernamuseet .se; Exercisplan 4; adult/under 18yr/concession Skr80/free/60, Stockholm Card free; ☼ 10am-8pm Tue, 10am-6pm Wed-Sun; ☒ 65; ♿

Cheeky and serious in equal measure, Stockholm's always-absorbing modern-art museum balances reliable crowd-pleasers like Robert Rauschenberg's *Monogram* with provocative new work from the likes of Paul McCarthy. Special exhibits in the basement are included with admission and always worth investigating, and if the boundary-testing art makes you feel light-headed, seek sustenance in the award-winning restaurant (p84).

### NORDISKA MUSEET

☎ 51 95 46 00; www.nordiskamuseet .se; Djurgårdsvägen 6-16; adult/under 19yr Skr70/free, Stockholm Card free; ☼ 10am-4pm Mon-Fri, 11am-5pm Sat & Sun Sep-May, 10am-5pm daily Jun-Aug; ☒ 47; ☒ 7

With its flouncy turrets and neo-Swedish Renaissance looks, Isak Gustav Clason's iconic building is hard to miss. Inside is a collection of all things Swedish, from Sami folklore to eclectic exhibitions of Swedish fashion, shoes, interiors and even table settings. The museum owns the largest collection of paintings by August Strindberg and the audio tours (Skr20) are nothing short of satisfying.

### ÖSTASIATISKA MUSEET

☎ 51 95 57 50; www.ostasiatiska.se; Tyghusplan; adult/under 19yr Skr60/free; ☼ 11am-8pm Tue, 11am-5pm Wed-Sun; ☒ 65; ♿

Know your Buddha from your bodhisattvas at Stockholm's Museum of Far Eastern Antiquities, famed for its world-class booty of ancient Eastern art, stoneware and porcelain. Particularly noteworthy is the collection of wares from the Chinese dynasties of Song, Ming and Qing, as well as the museum's fresh temporary shows, which cover anything from comic-book manga to the art of Japanese tattoos.

## PRINS EUGENS WALDEMARSUDDE

☎ 54 58 37 00; www.waldemarsudde .com; Prins Eugens väg 6; adult/under 19yr/concession Skr85/free/65, Stockholm Card free; ⏰ 11am-5pm Tue-Sun, to 8pm Thu; 🚌 47; 🚋 7

Dubbed 'the painter prince', Prins Eugens (1865–1947) once lived at this waterside villa, designed by Ferdinand Boberg, creator of the NK department store (p62). The property now houses the late prince's superlative collection of Nordic art, including works by Anders Zorn, Carl Larsson and Isaac Grünewald, as well as landscape paintings by the reclusive royal himself. The terraced garden boasts sculptures by Carl Milles and Auguste Rodin, sublimely matched by cool water views and an 18th-century windmill.

## SKANSEN

☎ 442 80 00; www.skansen.se; Djurgårdsslätten 49-51; adult Skr40-120, child Skr30-50, depending on season, Stockholm Card free; ⏰ 10am-8pm May–mid-Jun, 10am-10pm mid-Jun–Aug, 10am-5pm Sep, 10am-4pm Oct-Apr; 🚌 47; 🚋 7

This open-air museum (the world's oldest) is a one-stop tour of Sweden, featuring over 150 traditional buildings from across the country, including a Sami camp with reindeer. Artisans blow glass in historic workshops, bakers sell Scandi treats in vintage bakeries and Nordic animals roam the in-house zoo. For a glimpse of pygmy marmosets, the world's smallest monkeys, pop into

Old-time Swedish style at Skansen

the quirky **aquarium** ( ☎ 660 10 10; adult/child Skr80/45; ⏱ 10am-4pm Mon-Fri & 10am-5pm Sat & Sun Sep-Apr, 10am-5pm Mon-Fri & 10am-6pm Sat & Sun May, 10am-6pm Mon-Fri & 10am-7pm Sat & Sun early Jun–mid-Jun & mid-Aug–late Aug, 10am-8pm daily mid-Jun–early Aug, 10am-7pm daily early Aug–mid-Aug).

### SVENSK FORM

☎ 463 31 30; www.svenskform.se; Holmamiralens väg 2; admission Skr20; ⏱ 5-8pm Wed, noon-5pm Thu & Fri, noon-4pm Sat & Sun Sep-May, to 5pm Wed-Fri Jun-Aug; 🚌 65
Stockholm's foremost design centre features temporary exhibitions of cutting-edge industrial design and applied arts, and a Swedish design library and archive, as well as a cool little design shop and cafe, complete with copies of in-house design magazine *Form*. On Wednesday evenings, designers (and the design-inclined) drop in for a drink, a schmooze and regular design seminars.

### THIELSKA GALLERIET

☎ 662 58 84; www.thielska-galleriet .se; Sjötullsbacken 6; adult/child Skr60/40, Stockholm Card free; ⏱ noon-4pm Mon-Sat, 1-4pm Sun; 🚌 69
Scandi art fans come here for Anders Zorn's portraits and nudes, Carl Larsson's portraits, Bruno Liljefors' precisely rendered wild-life paintings, August Strindberg's wild landscapes, and Edvard Munch's paintings and sketches, which include an enormous portrait of Strindberg and one of the collection's former owner, tycoon Ernest Thiel. Originally Thiel's home, this island mansion was designed by Ferdinand Boberg, designer of Prins Eugens Waldemarsudde (opposite).

### VASAMUSEET

☎ 51 95 48 00; www.vasamuseet .se; Galärvarvsvägen 14; adult/child Skr95/50, Stockholm Card free; ⏱ 10am-5pm & to 8pm Wed Sep-May, 8.30am-6pm Jun-Aug; 🚊 47; 🚢 7; ♿
The mighty warship *Vasa*, 69m long, 160ft tall and pride of the Swedish crown, set off on her maiden voyage on 10 August 1628. Within minutes, she and her 100-member crew capsized and sank tragicomically to the bottom of Saltsjön. Painstakingly raised in 1961, the ship and its incredible wooden sculptures were re-assembled like a giant 14,000-piece jigsaw and housed in an amazing purpose-built space. Salvaged objects from the ship, including shoes, cannonballs and pillboxes, provide a vivid glimpse into the lives of 17th-century sailors, but none more so than the forensically reconstructed faces of the ill-fated passengers. Guided tours in English run hourly from

**Erika & Ulrika Larsson**
*Founders of Normal, independent book publishers*

**How did Normal come about?** We started because there were all these books…everywhere else there were lots of books for gay people, but not in Sweden. We're small, edgy, queer; we have a very selective list. **Who are some of your authors?** Ann-Charlotte Alverfors…she was a star during the 1970s when she was 18 but hadn't been heard of for many years. Her writing is always very angry but she does it beautifully. She's a revolutionary, the way she writes. There's also Alan Hollinghurst. Angela Carter. Anna Lytsy *(Mrs Freud and I)*. **Plans for the future?** We do readings and teas and release parties, but it's irregular. We participate in the first-Sunday-of-the-month event. We want to use this room to do more readings, in the autumn. And people can always just come knock on our door. **Stockholm favourites?** The lunches at El Mundo (p103). And the Roxy (p102) is great.

9.30am in summer and at least twice daily at other times.

# SHOP

They mightn't be shopping meccas, but both islands boast brilliant museum gift shops. In December, don't miss the Julmarknad (Christmas market) at Skansen for Nordic yuletide treats.

### ☐ JUNIBACKEN
*Children's Books & Gifts*

☎ 58 72 30 00; www.junibacken.se; Galärparken; ☼ 10am-5pm Tue-Sun Jan-May & Sep-Dec, 10am-5pm daily Jun & Aug, 9am-6pm daily Jul; 🚌 47; 🚊 7
The bookshop at Astrid Lindgren's theme park (p78) is a treasure trove of must-have children's books, from *Pippi Longstocking* in Arabic to *The Brothers Lionheart* in English. Pick up cheeky Karlsson dolls, DVDs and cute little art cards with storybook themes.

### ☐ MODERNA MUSEET
*Books & Design*

☎ 51 95 52 21; www.modernamuseet .se; Exercisplan 4; ☼ 10am-8pm Tue, 10am-6pm Wed-Sun; 🚌 65
Culturally inclined shoppers won't know where to begin (or end) at this fabulous gallery shop. There's enough art and design books to make a coffee table swoon, and the collection of posters, postcards, art kits and cool

designer knick-knacks will have you spring-cleaning your wallet in style.

### ☐ SKANSEN SHOP *Handicrafts*

☎ 442 82 68; Djurgårdsslätten 49-51; ☼ 11am-4pm Jan & Feb, 11am-5pm Mar, Apr & Oct-Dec, 11am-6pm May & Sep, 11am-7pm Jun-Aug; 🚌 47; 🚊 7
A good bet for a complete Swedish makeover. Come here for handmade lambswool mittens, glassware and pottery, adorable jars of cloudberry jam, Swedish art books, jewellery and garden tools for that archipelago summer cottage you're saving for.

# EAT

From an organic cafe in the woods to slick waterside stars, the dining scene here is chilled, unhurried and perfect for lazy lingering.

### ☐ BLÅ PORTEN CAFÉ *Cafe* €

☎ 663 87 59; Djurgårdsvägen 64; ☼ 11am-10pm Mon-Thu, 11am-7pm Fri-Sun; 🚌 47; 🚊 7
A good bet for lunch, Blå Porten is best on a sunny day when you can linger in the romantic garden courtyard. Sunshine or not, the gluttonous table of fresh cakes and pastries is a constant, happy test of your self control. Thankfully, many of Djurgården's museums are within rolling distance.

## WORTH THE TRIP

Designed by Konstfack Academy graduates and set in a converted suburban post office 100m north of the Telefonplan metro station, restaurant-bar **Landet** ( ☎ 41 01 93 20; www.lan det.nu in Swedish; Lm Ericssons Väg 27, Hägersten; ⌚ restaurant 11am-2pm Mon-Fri, 5pm-midnight Mon-Thu, 5pm-1am Fri & Sat, bar 8pm-midnight Wed & Thu, 8pm-1am Fri & Sat; Ⓜ Telefonplan) is a hit with Stockholm's design crowd. In the oh-so-now dining room, they nosh on award-winning Swedish-French grub before heading up to the burlesque-fabulous bar. Here, red velvet drapes, strung coloured lights and gold graphic wall art set the scene for anything from DJ-spun electronica and jazz to live indie acts and the odd performance-art piece. And if that wasn't enough, the cinnamon-laced orange tequila is simply divine.

### 🍴 LISA PÅ UDDEN
*Seafood* €€€
☎ 660 94 75; www.lisapaudden.se in Swedish; Biskopsvägen 7; ⌚ 11.30am-4pm Mon-Fri, noon-5pm Sat & Sun, to 11pm daily mid-Apr–mid-Sep; 🚌 47
Baby sister to venerable seafood restaurant Lisa Elmqvist (p119), this waterside hotspot serves up classic Swedish seafood like toast skagen garnished with trout roe and a divine kalix bleak roe. In the summertime, work up an appetite by catching the ferry here from Ny-broplan (Map p77, A1), getting off at Biskopsudden 10 minutes later.

### 🍴 MODERNA MUSEET
*Museum Restaurant* €€
☎ 51 95 62 91; www.modernamuseet .se; Exercisplan 4; ⌚ 11am-8pm Tue, 11am-5pm Wed-Sun; 🚌 65
Moderna Museet has turned itself into a foodie hotspot with its Marge-designed restaurant. Run by celebrity chef Malin Söderström,

it's split into cafeteria-style Brickan (Tray) and á la carte Duken (Table Cloth). Both serve sharp, global fare with a side of gorgeous city views. Book ahead for the weekend brunch sessions (noon to 2pm Saturday and Sunday).

### 🍴 ROSENDALS TRÄDGÅRD
*Cafe* €
☎ 54 58 12 70; www.rosendalstradgard .se in Swedish; Rosendalsterrassen 12; ⌚ 11am-4pm Tue-Sun Feb-Apr & Oct–mid-Dec, 11am-5pm Mon-Fri & 11am-6pm Sat & Sun May-Sep; 🚌 47; 🚋 7
A 15-minute walk from Hazelius-porten, virtuous Rosendals Trädgård is seasonal, salubrious and oh-so-loveable, with heavenly desserts and sandwiches, all organic and mostly made with produce from the garden. Devour flaky fruit pastries under the apple trees or, if the weather's ugly, skulk around the greenhouses, look moody and pretend you're Strindberg.

# ⭐ PLAY

## 🟦 DJURGÅRDSBRONS SJÖCAFÉ *Canoe & Boat Hire*
☎ 661 44 88; Galärvarvsvägen 2;
🕓 summer 9am-9pm

Seeing Stockholm by water is fantastic, and it's something every visitor should do if time permits. This waterside cafe rents canoes, kayaks, rowboats and pedal boats for a fix of summertime bliss.

## 🟦 GRÖNA LUND TIVOLI
*Amusement Park*
☎ 58 75 01 00; www.gronalund .com in Swedish; Lilla Allmänna Gränd 9; adult/under 7yr & seniors Skr70/free, adults in Jul Skr80; 🕓 Thu-Sun May & mid-Aug–mid-Sep, daily Jun–mid-Aug, hours vary, check website; 🚌 47; 🚋 7

This landmark amusement park boasts Europe's tallest 'Free Fall', dropping thrillseekers 80m in two seconds. Children (and the sane)

have plenty of options and all rides except the Haunted House (Skr40) are covered by Gröna Lund Tivoli's ride coupon scheme (Skr20 per coupon); individual rides range from one to four coupons each. For unlimited access, buy a Skr260 day pass.

## 🟦 MODERNA DANSTEATERN
*Contemporary Dance*
☎ 611 32 33; www.modernadansteat ern.se; Slupskjulsvägen 32; adult/ under 18yr/concession & under 26yr Skr180/60/100; 🕓 varies; 🚌 65

If you like your moves sharp, abstract and boldly postmodern, head straight to this hothouse of experimental dance. Set in an ex-torpedo-making factory, this little theatre is one Stockholm's best bets for edgy new work from choreographers such as Satoshi Kudo, Susanne Jaresand and Anna Källblad.

---

### MELODIFESTIVALEN

Take reality TV series *Idol*, shoot it up with *schlager* (camp Swedish pop) and you have Melodifestivalen, Sweden's cultish annual song comp. Since 1959, Nordic songbirds have battled it out on the Melodifestivalen stage for the dubious honour of representing Sweden in the Eurovision Song Contest.

The nail-biting final takes place at Stockholm's Globen Arena every March. In 2006 an estimated TV audience of 4.6 million (almost half Sweden's entire population) watched veteran entrant and *schlager* queen Carola Häggkvist win with 'Evighet'.

The greatest ever win, however, remains that of 1974, when a fresh-faced foursome called ABBA wowed with 'Waterloo' before scooping Sweden's first-ever Eurovision victory. To see it live, see p22.

# >SÖDERMALM & LÅNGHOLMEN

Take a pinch of eccentricity, a splash of laid-back cool, sprinkle over an inner-city island and you have Södermalm. This former working-class district is now the city's creative engine room – a latte-laced mix of experimental art, gritty bars and retro chic.

According to legend, child-snatching witches once took off from Södermalm's soaring northern cliffs, bound for mythical Blåkulla. The witches may have gone, but the views remain bewitching. Add to this a lip-smacking restaurant scene and attitude-free nightlife, and you'll soon see why 'Söder' is Stockholm's favourite hangout.

While Götgatan and trendy SoFo (the area south of Folkungagatan) keep the fashion-savvy drooling, grungy Hornstull packs a punch with its indie hangouts and edgy vibe.

The languid island of Långholmen, connected to Södermalm by bridge, once housed the notorious Kronohäktet prison, Sweden's largest jail. The prison is now a youth hostel and the island's beaches are the summer domain of bronzed Swedish sun slaves.

Heaving with hip fashion: the Brunogallerian mall (p93)

# SÖDERMALM & LÅNGHOLMEN

## 🔵 SEE

| | |
|---|---|
| Almgrens Sidenväveri Museum ........................1 | E2 |
| Hornstull Strand ............2 | B3 |
| Katarina Kyrka ...............3 | F3 |
| Katarinahissen ..............4 | F2 |
| Leksaksmuseet ...........(see 6) | |
| Maria Magdalena Kyrka ..........................5 | E2 |
| Spårvägsmuseet ...........6 | H4 |
| Stockholms Stadsmuseum ...........7 | E2 |

## 🔲 SHOP

| | |
|---|---|
| 10 Swedish Designers ....................8 | F2 |
| Acne .............................9 | F3 |
| Blås & Knåda ...............10 | E2 |
| Brunogallerian ...........11 | E3 |
| Chokladfabriken .........12 | G3 |
| DesignTorget ...............13 | F3 |
| Efva Attling ................14 | E2 |
| Gina Tricot .................15 | E2 |
| Grandpa .....................16 | F3 |
| Hallongrottan .............17 | A3 |
| Handtryckta Tapeter ...................18 | A2 |
| Judits Herr .................19 | D2 |

| | |
|---|---|
| Judits Second Hand .....20 | D2 |
| Konsthantverkana .......21 | E2 |
| Lisa Larssons ...............22 | G3 |
| Nitty Gritty .................23 | D2 |
| Pet Sounds Records .....24 | F3 |
| Press Stop ...................(see 13) | |
| Sivletto .......................25 | G4 |
| Sneakersnstuff ...........26 | F3 |
| Tea Centre of Stockholm .................27 | E2 |
| Tjallamalla ..................28 | G3 |

## 🍴 EAT

| | |
|---|---|
| Café Lillavi ..................29 | F3 |
| Chutney ......................30 | F3 |
| Créperie Fyra Knop ......31 | F2 |
| Hermans Trädgårdscafé .........32 | G2 |
| Hornstulls Mjölkbar ....33 | A2 |
| Ho's ............................34 | B3 |
| Jerusalem Kebab .........35 | F3 |
| Koh Phangan ...............36 | F3 |
| Nystekt Strömming ......37 | F2 |
| Ösgöta Källaren ...........38 | F3 |
| Pelikan ......................39 | F4 |
| Roxy ...........................40 | G4 |
| Svart Kaffe .................41 | F3 |
| Yu Love Bibimbab .......42 | G3 |

## 🍸 DRINK

| | |
|---|---|
| Akkurat .......................43 | E2 |
| Bara Vi .......................44 | F3 |
| El Mundo ....................45 | G3 |
| Eriks Gondolen ...........46 | F2 |
| Kvarnen ......................47 | F3 |
| Nada ...........................48 | F3 |
| Pet Sounds Bar ...........49 | F4 |
| Rival ...........................50 | E2 |

## ⭐ PLAY

| | |
|---|---|
| Bio Rio .......................51 | A3 |
| Debaser ......................52 | F2 |
| Debaser Medis ............53 | F3 |
| Eriksdalsbadet ............54 | F5 |
| Folkoperan .................55 | D2 |
| Iglo Ljuscafe ...............56 | A3 |
| Lady Patricia ..............57 | F2 |
| Liljeholmsbadet ..........58 | A3 |
| Marie Laveau ..............59 | D2 |
| Mosebacke Etablissement ...........60 | F2 |
| Södra Teatern .............61 | F2 |

Please see over for map

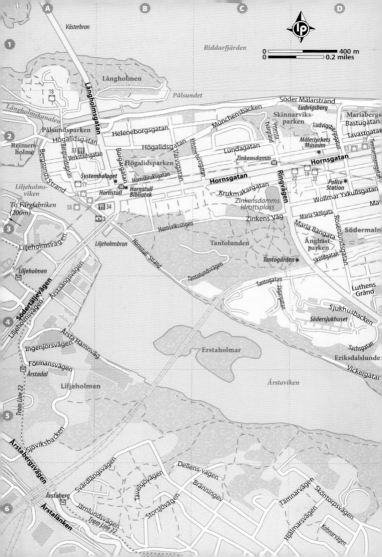

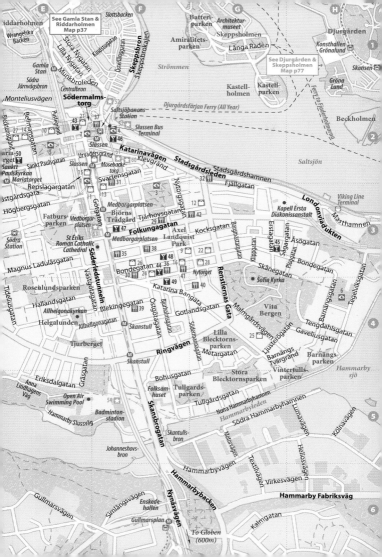

#  SEE

## ALMGRENS SIDENVÄVERI MUSEUM

☎ 642 56 16; www.kasiden.se; Repslagargatan 15; adult/under 12yr Skr65/free, Stockholm Card free; ⏱ 10am-4pm Mon-Fri, 11am-3pm Sat; Ⓜ Slussen; ♿

Knut August Almgren founded this historic weaving factory in 1883 using parts of a Jacquard loom smuggled from France in barrels of cognac. (The art of Jacquard weave looming was a guarded French secret, forcing the crafty Almgren to pose as a Frenchman in order to learn, and steal, the craft.) It's now an adorable working museum; you can watch the weavers work the original Jacquard looms between 10am and 3pm Monday to Thursday, learn about Sweden's silk weaving history and swoon over shimmering fabrics. The museum shop is Stockholm's best bet for hand-woven products.

## HORNSTULL STRAND

☎ 658 63 50; www.hornstullstrand.se; Hornstull Strand; ⏱ 9am-midnight Sun-Thu, to 2am Fri & Sat; Ⓜ Hornstull

Though it's no longer home to the cool street market formerly known as Street, this area – a casual assemblage of riverfront cafes and terraces with a warehouse space and nightclub – usually has something going on at all hours, whether it's a vintage flea market or a line of food carts or an impromptu motorcycle rally. Check the website for a schedule.

## KATARINA KYRKA

☎ 743 68 00; www.svkyrkankatarina .com in Swedish; Högbergsgatan; admission free; ⏱ 11am-5pm Mon-Fri, 10am-5pm Sat & Sun; Ⓜ Medborgarplatsen

Designed by Jean de la Vallée and completed in 1695, the sublimely beautiful Katarina Kyrka stands on the 1520 burial site of the Stockholm Bloodbath victims – the betrayed Swedish nobility trapped, beheaded and burnt for opposing King Christian II's Danish invasion. The church itself caught fire in 1723. After it was restored, history repeated itself in 1990 when fire brought down the cupola. It's since been painstakingly

---

### VINTAGE LIGHTS & PEARLY WHITES

In the cluster of neon signs above Slussen you'll spot a flashing advertisement for Stomatol toothpaste. Originally located on the Katarinahissen elevator (right), this giant tube of toothpaste has been squeezing its contents onto a twinkling toothbrush since 1906. It consists of 1361 coloured light bulbs, and legend has it that the flashing flow of toothpaste made horses rear in fright.

Gliding past beautiful Katarina Kyrka

reconstructed using 17th-century building methods. Assassinated foreign minister Anna Lindh lies buried in its leafy cemetery. Organ music fills the church at noon on Tuesday and Thursday.

### KATARINAHISSEN
☎ 642 47 85; Slussen; adult/under 7yr/under 15yr Skr10/free/5; ☽ 10am-6pm Sep–mid-May, 8am-10pm mid-May–Aug; Ⓜ Slussen

Get high (literally) with a trip to the top of this industrial-age show-off. Connecting Slussen to the lofty Söder cliffs, the original 1883 steam lift was replaced with a less romantic model in 1936. Still, the views remain striking and the sky-high Eriks Gondolen bar and restaurant (p103) remains one

of Stockholm's best places to sip, sup and swoon. For a free ride to the top, take the lift inside the adjacent Konsum/Coop building and walk across the elevated bridge.

### MARIA MAGDALENA KYRKA
☎ 462 29 40; Hornsgatan 21; admission free; ☽ 11am-5pm Thu-Mon, 11am-7.30pm Wed; Ⓜ Slussen

Consecrated in 1643, Södermalm's oldest church stands on the site of a 14th-century chapel, torn down by serial church trasher Gustav Vasa after the Reformation of 1527. Although fire destroyed much of the current building in 1759, it was faithfully rebuilt, including the transept designed by Nicodemus Tessin the Elder and a beautiful stone entrance portal by Tessin the Younger. Pop inside to see the *Adoration of the Shepherds* altarpiece painting (dating from around 1800) and the richly rococo-style pulpit. Come at 12.15pm on Thursday for free organ music.

### SPÅRVÄGSMUSEET
☎ 686 17 60; www.sparvagsmuseet.sl.se in Swedish; Tegelviksgatan 22; adult/under 7yr/concession & under 19yr Skr30/free/15, Stockholm Card free; ☽ 10am-5pm Mon-Fri, 11am-4pm Sat & Sun; ▣ 2

Board a 1938 bus, hop on a retro metro carriage, or create your own computer-generated public-transit network at this surprisingly cool

## GARBO & THE CITY

It was at Blekingegatan 32 (Map pp88–9, F4) that Swedish screen queen Greta Garbo (1905–90) spent her childhood, in a cramped one-bedroom apartment. The building may have gone, but a plaque commemorates the fact, as does a bronze bust of the star on the corner of Blekingegatan and Tjurebergsgatan.

Across town on Hötorget (Map pp52–3, F5), a young Garbo (then Greta Lovisa Gustafsson) worked as a salesgirl and catalogue model at PUB, and studied drama at Kungliga Dramatiska Teatern (p123), before a role in director Mauritz Stiller's 1924 film *Gösta Berlings saga* (The Atonement of Gösta Berling) led her to Hollywood a year later.

Stockholm's Grand Hôtel (p146) eventually became the reclusive icon's home away from home, where she'd hide in the bathroom while the hotel floor manager delivered her dinner. According to private letters released in 2005 to mark the centenary of her birth, Garbo's antisocial tendencies were partly fuelled by self-obsession, depression and shame over her latrine-cleaning father. In 1999, nine years after her death in New York, the sultry siren's ashes were interred in section 12 of Skogskyrkogården (p49).

transport museum. This former bus depot is also home to toy museum **Leksaksmuseet** ( ☎ 641 61 00; www.leksaksmuseet.se; adult/child/concession Skr30/free/15; ☽ 10am-5pm Mon-Fri, 11am-4pm Sat & Sun), an oversized fantasy nursery packed with everything you probably ever wanted as a child (and may still hanker after as an adult).

### ◙ STOCKHOLMS STADSMUSEUM

☎ 50 83 16 20; www.stadsmuseum.stockholm.se; Ryssgården, Slussen; admission free; ☽ 11am-5pm Tue-Sun, 11am-8pm Thu; Ⓜ Slussen; ♿

History gets a multisensory makeover at the brilliant Stockholm City Museum, housed in a building designed by Nicodemus Tessin the Elder and once used as a dungeon.

Inside, a time-line exhibition traces Stockholm's development from fortified port to modern metropolis via plague, fire and good old-fashioned scandal. You can smell medieval potions, peek into an 18th-century tavern and lust at the legendary Lohe Treasure, 20kg of 18th-century silver discovered in 1937. The temporary exhibitions are nothing short of refreshing, from Johan Hagelbäck's 'Raisin Art' to the culture of death in Stockholm.

## SHOP

Söder's shopping spine is Götgatan (Map pp88–9, F4), home to a few legendary design shops. For uberhip local threads, pound the pavements of SoFo (Map pp88–9, F3).

## 🏠 10 SWEDISH DESIGNERS
*Design*

☎ 643 25 04; www.tiogruppen. com; Götgatan 25; 🕐 11am-6.30pm Mon-Fri, 11am-5pm Sat, noon-4pm Sun; Ⓜ Slussen

Tiogruppen was started in 1970 by a group of then-maverick textile artists, and its bold geometric patterns have become icons of modern Swedish design. Forget white-on-white Scandi minimalism; from the tote bags and cushions to the plates and napkins, the look is shamelessly bright and refreshingly bombastic.

## 🏠 ACNE *Fashion*

☎ 611 64 11; Nytorgsgatan 36; 🕐 noon-7pm Mon-Fri, to 4pm Sat; Ⓜ Medborgarplatsen

This outpost of the designer jeans brand was designed by Acne architect Andreas Fornell, allegedly with inspiration from Pablo Picasso's art studio. There are other locations scattered around town, all equally chic and intimidating.

## 🏠 BLÅS & KNÅDA *Design*

☎ 642 77 67; www.blasknada.se; Hornsgatan 26; 🕐 11am-6pm Tue-Fri, 11am-4pm Sat, noon-4pm Sun; Ⓜ Slussen

Glass and ceramics are the main attraction at this venerable seasoned gallery. Run by around 45 Swedish potters and glassblowers who take turns manning the floor, it's a good

Shoppers chilling at hot Brunogallerian

place for 'Where-did-you-get-that?' sculptures, vases and dishes, as well as art books and cards to top off the perfect gift.

## 🏠 BRUNOGALLERIAN
*Fashion & Design*

☎ 757 76 00; www.brunogotgatsback en.se; Götgatan 36; 🕐 11am-7pm Mon-Fri, 11am-5pm Sat, noon-4pm Sun; Ⓜ Slussen

Further proof of Söder's dreads-to-design gentrification, this hotshot mini-mall houses some of Stockholm's coolest fashion labels, including Whyred, Way, Stuk and Filippa K. Try on some of the sleek-and-shiny, futuristic frocks at Miss Sixty.

## SOFO

Although grungy Hornstull is sneaking up on SoFo as Stockholm's hippest 'hood, this pocket of self-conscious cool still leads the pack with its cutting-edge fashion boutiques and indie-chic cafes and bars.

Loosely bordered by Folkungagatan to the north, Götgatan to the west, Renstiernas Gata to the east and Ringvägen to the south (hence the acronym SOuth of FOlkungsgatan), it's where you'll find fashion-forward Tjallamalla (p99) and Stockholm's coolest shoe shop SneakersnStuff (p98). Raid the racks at Pet Sounds Records (p97), then nosh and slosh the night away in the fab little bars on Skånegatan.

The last Thursday of every month is SoFo Nights, when many shops open till 9pm and in-store gigs range from DJ sets to fashion shows. Check www.sofo.se for details.

### CHOKLADFABRIKEN
*Chocolate*

☎ 640 05 68; www.chokladfabriken
.com; Renstiernas Gata 12; ⏰ 10am-
6.30pm Mon-Fri, 10am-5pm Sat; 🚌 3
Cocoa addicts swear by this savvy chocolate peddler, whose head chocolatier Martin Isaksson trained at the *Maison du Chocolat* in Paris. Bite into the cardamom praline and you'll be hooked. One line of chocolates features artwork by graphic designer Katy Kimbell, and the regular evening tasting sessions (Skr320, 90 minutes) are coveted affairs (book two to three months ahead). Best of all, you can kick back in the adjoining cafe and succumb to Stockholm's dreamiest hot chocolate (made with 70% cocoa dark chocolate). There's also a branch in Norrmalm (p60) and another one in Östermalm on Grevgatan 37.

### DESIGNTORGET *Design*

☎ 462 35 20; www.designtorget.se; Götgatan 31; ⏰ 10am-7pm Mon-Fri, 10am-
5pm Sat, noon-4pm Sun; Ⓜ Slussen
DesignTorget collects the work of design-scene up-and-comers and sells it alongside the work of established denizens. From resin rings to cutting-edge candlesticks, you won't leave empty-handed. There are other outlets at **Kulturhu-
set** (Map pp52-3; ☎ 21 91 50), **Nybrogatan 16** (Map pp110-11, B4; ☎ 611 53 03), and inside **Västermalmsgallerian** (Map p127; ☎ 33 11 53), Kungsholmen. Götgatan 31 is also home to **Press Stop** ( ☎ 644 35 10; ⏰ 10am-7pm Mon-Fri, 10am-5pm Sat, noon-5pm Sun), Stock-holm's best news stand for design and fashion magazines.

### EFVA ATTLING *Jewellery*

☎ 642 99 49; www.efvaattlingstock
holm.com; Hornsgatan 44; ⏰ 10am-6pm
Mon-Fri, 11am-3pm Sat; Ⓜ Mariatorget

At first Efva Attling was a model, then a singer in a band called the X-Models. Now she's even more famous as one of Sweden's funkiest silversmiths. Her designs are clean-cut and stunning, with names like Homo Sapiens and Make Love Not War. Accessorise with a pair of Efva Attling sunglasses (as worn by Lisa Marie Presley).

###  GINA TRICOT Clothing

☎ 642 02 59; Götgatan 30; ⏰ 9am-7pm Mon-Fri, noon-4pm Sat; Ⓜ Slussen

At the time of writing, this cavernous discount fashion emporium, along the lines of H&M, was the fastest-growing clothing chain in Scandinavia. Check it out for budget versions of haute couture or simple T-shirts, accessories and cotton basics.

Retro chic on SoFo's streets

### 🛍 GRANDPA Concept Store

☎ 643 60 80; www.grandpa.se in Swedish; Södermannagatan 21; ⏰ 11.30am-6.30pm Mon-Fri, noon-4pm Sat & Sun; Ⓜ Medborgarplatsen

Bag everything from vintage boots and retro radios to gritty art books (and local art). Best of the lot are the yummy local threads from the likes of Hope, House of Dagmar, Stylein and rising star Fifth Avenue Shoe Repair, whose own boutique is a short strut away at Bondegatan 46.

### 📖 HALLONGROTTAN Books

☎ 658 13 20; www.hallongrottan .com in Swedish; Bergsundsgatan 25; ⏰ noon-7pm Tue-Fri, noon-5pm Sat & Sun; Ⓜ Hornstull

Adding weight to Hornstull's counter-culture rep, this queer-centric bookshop boasts an eclectic mix of gay and feminist titles, queer-friendly kids books, trashy zombie flicks and free hallongrottan (raspberry tartlets). In-store cultural gigs range from screenings of Pink Flamingos to readings by scribes like Sarah Waters and Dennis Cooper – check the website for details.

### 🏠 HANDTRYCKTA TAPETER Wallpaper

☎ 720 52 90; www.handtrycktatapeter .se; Knaperstavägen 7A; ⏰ by appointment; Ⓜ Hornstull

**Jennifer Spratly**
*Food anthropologist and longtime Stockholmer now studying in Hong Kong*

**What do you miss when you're away?** I miss good-looking, mature, open-hearted, critically thinking, independent Scandinavian men (my sweetheart included). I miss Stockholm masculinity. Not the Viking approach to things (loud-mouthed, drunk, setting things on fire), but just the sight of men on parental leave with kids in strollers, for instance. Stockholm tells me there are many ways to perform manhood, which I believe is unique. **When you return?** At Bondens Matbod (www.bondensmatbod.se) in Hötorgshallen, I buy a piece of 'Ebba Grön' cheese (named after a renowned Swedish rock band in the '80s), made by Ebba the cow up north, and put it on a slice of fruit bread. It's a hit! **Has your perspective changed since spending time in HK?** Stockholm wants to be Manhattan, and when people come to visit us they say it's adorable. By international standards, service culture sucks. Think 'ambitious village'. **Where do you take visitors?** For culinary experiences in pastoral settings we bring people to the outlying islands Utö and Oaxen. Also people-watching and sunbathing at City Hall (Stadshuset, p128). **How's the restaurant scene?** Modern Swedish high-end cuisine has become magically creative in the past few years, and the increased use of local products tells me restaurants aim to restore a sense of pride in the 'Nordic way of life', which is fairly new.

With a fan base including royalty, museums and retro-loving stylistas, this artisan wallpaper studio reproduces rare and vintage Swedish and foreign wallpapers using authentic handmade methods. The owner and her colleague run tours of the space, and it's always best to call ahead.

### JUDITS SECOND HAND
*Vintage Fashion*

☎ 84 45 10; www.judits.se; Hornsgatan 75; ⏲ 11am-7pm Mon, 11am-6pm Tue-Fri, 11am-4pm Sat; Ⓜ Zinkensdamm

Style meister and boutique owner Christian Quaglia scours the markets of Italy to bring back the goods – 1960s and 1970s haute hip. Up the street, his latest venture **Judits Herr** (Hornsgatan 65) keeps the guys looking dapper in classic Italian loafers, vintage brimmed hats and sexy Acne denim.

### KONSTHANTVERKANA
*Design*

☎ 611 03 70; www.konsthantverkana .se; Södermalmstorg 4; ⏲ 11am-6pm Mon-Fri, 11am-4pm Sat; Ⓜ Slussen

Rumour has it that the Swedish royals shop here and, quite frankly, we don't blame them. Run by a union of 166 Swedish designers and artists, this revamped gallery-cum-shop is the stuff *Wallpaper* magazine dreams are made of – think sublime silver rings,

loft-worthy ceramics, too-cool crockery and seductive textiles.

### LISA LARSSONS
*Secondhand Vintage Fashion*

☎ 643 61 53; Bondegatan 48; ⏲ noon-6pm Tue-Fri, noon-3pm Sat; Ⓜ Medborgarplatsen

This microscopic shop is jam-packed with a super-fine collection of vintage clothes and accessories. It's a '50s to '70s thing, with everything from rock-around-the-clock frocks and skirts to disco chic and sexy leather jackets.

### NITTY GRITTY
*Concept Store*

☎ 24 00 44; www.nittygritty.se in Swedish; Krukmakargatan 24-26; ⏲ 11am-6pm Mon-Fri, 11am-5pm Sat, noon-4pm Sun; Ⓜ Zinkensdamm

Head here for international catwalk threads, shoes and accessories from icons like Miu Miu, Prada, Fred Perry and Dupe, as well as Håkansson cosmetics, French champagne, cult DVDs and offbeat toys like President Nixon action dolls. It has an in-store hair salon and a cafe (the Bloody Mary soup is bloody brilliant), and there's a cheaper outlet next door.

### PET SOUNDS RECORDS
*Music & Books*

☎ 702 97 98; www.petsounds.se; Skånegatan 53; ⏲ 11am-7pm Mon-Fri,

## WORTH THE TRIP

For a suburban treasure hunt, dive into the much-loved **Skärholmen flea market** ( ☎ 710 00 60; www .loppmarknaden.se in Swedish; bottom floor of Skärholmen Centrum parking garage; admission free Mon-Fri, Skr15 Sat, Skr10 Sun, free after 3pm Sat & Sun; 🕑 11am-6pm Mon-Fri, 9am-4pm Sat, 11am-4pm Sun; Ⓜ Skärholmen), where vendors flog everything from Swedish rocking chairs to Pakistani videos; there's also an African beauty shop that stocks Eritrean and Ethiopian music, a fab fabric shop and a Caribbean tarot-card reader, all in a gigantic, un-assuming basement.

11am-5pm Sat, 1-5pm Sun; Ⓜ Medbor-garplatsen
No cute puppies here, just kick-ass music. Please your ears with every-thing from indie and alt-rock to pop, techno, rock and kitsch Latin pop. Pick up cult art books, concert tickets and flyers, or simply pick the staff's brains over espresso at the tiny in-house bar. For late-night tunes, hit sister venue Pet Sounds Bar (p104) across the street.

### 🔲 SIVLETTO Vintage
☎ 643 39 72; www.sivletto.com; Malm-gårdsvägen 16-18; 🕑 noon-7pm Tue-Thu, noon-6pm Fri, noon-4pm Sat & Sun; 🚌 3
Live out your Back to the Future fantasy at this super-secret ode

to midcentury cool. Hidden away in a basement at the bottom of a claustrophobic staircase, behind an anonymous door, on an out-of-the-way street, this sprawling retro emporium boasts a diner-style cafe, a Jimmy Dean barber and enough 1950s fashion, furnishings and nostalgia to bring out the Fonz or Sandra Dee within.

### 🔲 SNEAKERSNSTUFF Sneakers
☎ 743 03 22; www.sneakersnstuff .com; Åsögatan 124; 🕑 11am-6.30pm Mon-Fri, noon-5pm Sat, noon-3pm Sun; Ⓜ Medborgarplatsen
Funk-up your feet with exclusive and limited-edition sneakers from brands like And 1, Tretorn and US vintage brand PF Flyers. Look out for specially commissioned numbers, and match them up with DJ-designed threads from New York's Staple, Baltimore's Milkcrate and LA's Mixwell. DJs play the oc-casional Saturday set and there's an in-store cafe to boot.

### 🔲 TEA CENTRE OF STOCKHOLM Tea
☎ 640 42 10; www.teacentre.se; Hornsgatan 46; 🕑 9.30am-6pm Mon-Fri, 10am-4pm Sat Sep-Apr, to 2pm Sat May-Aug; Ⓜ Mariatorget
This dark, heavenly scented tea shop is the place to buy Söder-blandning, a hit in Japan and Söder's very own blend of tea. If

sweet and fruity isn't your thing, there are another 200-odd blends to choose from, as well as jars of velvety lemon curd, marmalade and buttery Scottish shortbread for a perfect afternoon tea.

### 🔲 TJALLAMALLA *Fashion*
☎ 640 78 47; www.tjallamalla.com; Bondegatan 46; ⏰ noon-6pm Mon-Fri, noon-4pm Sat; Ⓜ Medborgarplatsen
If you don't know Tjallamalla in Stockholm, you're fashion illiterate. This is *the* place for hot men's and women's rookie labels like Very Truly Yours, Whipping Floyd and JA! Graduates from the city's prestigious Beckmans College of Design sometimes sell their collections here on commission.

## 🍴 EAT
The food options in Söder, like anything in this artsy part of town, are just a little more offbeat and individualistic than elsewhere. Whether you opt for Sami, Korean or vegan, chances are it'll be a little easier on the wallet too.

### 🍴 CAFÉ LILLAVI *Cafe* €
☎ 073641254; Folkungagatan 73; ⏰ 8am-6pm Mon-Thu, 10am-6pm Sat, noon-6pm Sun; Ⓜ Medborgarplatsen
Set in a sidewalk kiosk, this cute-as-a-button cafe is run by two chatty friends, Therece and Victoria, and Victoria's dad, Mats. Choose a table (there are two), sit on a sheepskin chair and tackle Victoria's aunt's devilish chocolate cake. Of course, the virtuous can always opt for the organic Thai pie served with homemade mash and red-wine sauce.

### 🍴 CHUTNEY *Vegetarian* €€
☎ 640 30 10; www.chutney.se; Katarina Bangata 19; ⏰ 11am-10pm Mon-Fri, noon-10pm Sat & Sun; Ⓜ Medborgarplatsen; Ⓥ

---

### LIGHT'NING THE LOAD
In a country infamous for its long dark winters, it's not surprising that an estimated 80% of Swedes suffer from winter depression, or the aptly named SAD (Seasonal Affective Disorder). One victim, Martin Sylwan, has turned its treatment into a trendy social event with his bright white **Iglo Ljuscafé** (Light Cafe; ☎ 668 82 70; www.iglo.se; Hornstull Strand 1; admission 1hr Skr110, incl breakfast Skr160, cash only; ⏰ 7am-2pm Mon, Wed & Fri, 7am-2pm & 4-8pm Tue & Thu, 10am-5pm Sat & Sun, closed mid-May–Sep; Ⓜ Hornstull). Ergonomically designed and awash with melatonin-kicking neon, this luminous lounge offers one-hour light treatments, with the added options of organic **breakfasts** ( ⏰ 7am-11am Mon-Fri, 10am-1pm Sat & Sun), sandwiches and Amazonian sorbet.

Left-leaning, boho-inclined Chutney feeds the arty masses on inspired vegetarian and vegan creations like potato pancakes, coconut stews and rich mushroom ravioli. The Skr75 lunch menu (11am to 5pm daily), with its generous helpings and divine homemade breads, is good value. Wash it all down with a glass of organic red.

### 🍴 CRÊPERIE FYRA KNOP
*Crêpes* €
☎ 640 77 27; Svartensgatan 4; ⏱ 5-11pm Mon-Fri, 11.30am-11pm Sat & Sun; Ⓜ Slussen

This Söder stalwart serves up perfect crêpes in an intimate dive with a hint of shantytown chic – think reggae tunes and old tin billboards for Stella Artois. Give in to the Grand Marnier, orange marmalade and dark chocolate combo and don't be surprised if you find yourself licking that plate clean.

### 🍴 HERMANS TRÄDGÅRDSCAFÉ *Vegetarian* €
☎ 643 94 80; www.hermans.se; Fjällgatan 23A; ⏱ 11am-9pm, to 11pm Jun-Aug; 🚌 3; Ⓥ

The cakes aren't always brilliant, but the vegetarian buffets here are unvaryingly fab. Get your aura glowing with soul-satisfying lasagne, stuffed vine leaves,

crunchy potato wedges and Moroccan-inspired salads served in the barrel-vaulted basement or on the swoon-worthy summer terrace, complete with sea and city views.

### 🍴 HORNSTULLS MJÖLKBAR
*Cafe* €
☎ 668 08 70; www.mjolkbaren.com in Swedish; Verkstadsgatan 10; ⏱ 9am-6pm Mon-Fri, 10am-5pm Sat & Sun; Ⓜ Hornstull

This little hangout is pure Hornstull hip – think Dietrich on the turntable, Damon Albarn–styled staff, and an eclectic mix of vintage-clad students, script-clutching actors and the odd Dita Von Teese wannabe. The grub is simple and good (toasties, soups and smoothies) and the weekend brunch is a perfect prelude to lazy afternoon ambling at nearby Hornstull Strand (p90).

### 🍴 HO'S *Chinese* €€
☎ 84 44 20; Hornsgatan 151; ⏱ noon-10.30pm Tue-Thu, noon-11pm Fri, 12.30-11pm Sat, 12.30-10.30pm Sun; Ⓜ Hornstull

Despite the name, this no-fuss joint serves up respectable Cantonese/Sichuan cooking. Matriarch Ho Yuk Yee's dumplings are divine, and usually the first thing to run out, so get in early or request them a day ahead.

## WORTH THE TRIP

Contemporary art fiends drool over **Färgfabriken** ( ☎ 645 07 07; www.fargfabriken.se; Lövholmsbrinken 1, Liljeholmen; adult/concession Skr40/30, Stockholm Card free; ⏰ 11am-4pm Wed-Sun during exhibitions; Ⓜ Liljeholmen; ♿). The place that once made lawn-mowers now makes headlines with its leading exhibitions – indeed, the New York Art Forum named this hub for contemporary art and architecture one of the world's best galleries. Check listings or the website for opening hours and upcoming shows and seminars (filmmaker David Lynch once exhibited here) and don't miss the chance to rub shoulders at an opening party.

### 🍴 JERUSALEM KEBAB
*Kebabs* €

☎ 644 39 82; Götgatan 59; ⏰ 9am-late; Ⓜ Medborgarplatsen

It's not fancy, but Jerusalem Kebab has earned its reputation for churning out awesome kebabs at all hours of the day and night, particularly the wee ones. Finding affordable and decent grub in Stockholm after 10pm can be a challenge, so this hole in the wall provides a most welcome service.

### 🍴 KOH PHANGAN *Thai* €€€

☎ 642 68 65; www.kohphangan.nu; Skånegatan 57; ⏰ 11am-1am Mon-Fri, 2pm-1am Sat & Sun; Ⓜ Medborgarplatsen

A gay cruising venue in a previous life, this outrageously kitsch Thai restaurant has to be seen to be believed. Chow down *pad thai* in a real tuk-tuk to the accompanying racket of crickets and a tropical thunderstorm, or take on the fiery red curry at a glass-covered bathtub complete

with bubbles. Book ahead or wait an hour.

### 🍴 NYSTEKT STRÖMMING
*Swedish* €

**Södermalmstorg;** ⏰ lunch & dinner; Ⓜ Slussen

As you'd expect from its name (Newly Fried Herring), you'll get some of the best fried herring in Stockholm from this little caravan outside the Tunnelbana station at Slussen.

### 🍴 ÖSTGÖTA KÄLLAREN
*French-Swedish-Mediterranean* €€

☎ 643 22 40; Östgötagatan 41; ⏰ 11.30am-1am, kitchen closes 11.30pm; Ⓜ Medborgarplatsen

The regulars at this soulful pub-restaurant are a varied bunch; they range from pierced rockers to blue-rinse grandmas, all smitten with the dimly lit romantic atmosphere, amiable vibe and hearty Swedish, Eastern European and French-Med grub.

**PELIKAN** *Swedish* €€€

☎ 55 60 90 92; www.pelikan.se; Blekingegatan 40; ⏰ 3.30pm-1am Mon-Thu, 1pm-1am Fri-Sun, minimum age 23yr; Ⓜ Skanstull

High ceilings, wood-panelling and no-nonsense waiters in waistcoats set the scene for classic *husmanskost* (traditional Swedish fare) at this century-old beer hall. The superb menu includes an assortment of herring and cheeses and expertly roasted spare-ribs served with red cabbage and apple purée. Add huge beer glasses and you're set for an epic toast to Sverige.

**ROXY**
*Fusion/Mediterranean* €€€

☎ 640 96 55; www.roxysofo.se in Swedish; Nytorget 6; ⏰ 5-11pm Tue & Sun, 5pm-midnight Wed & Thu, 5pm-1am Fri & Sat; Ⓜ Skanstull

Laid-back but never short on chic, Roxy draws an erudite mix of lipstick lesbians, publishing types and Söder-style socialites, all smitten with modern-Med mains and tapas treats (think soy-marinated tuna with mango). Roll in some tango tunes, the odd brusque Spanish waitress, and all that's missing is Frida Kahlo at the bar.

**SVART KAFFE** *Cafe* €

☎ 462 95 00; Södermannagatan 23; ⏰ 8am-4pm Mon-Fri, 10am-7pm Sat & Sun; Ⓜ Medborgarplatsen

Smack bang in SoFo (see boxed text, p94), this hole-in-the-wall cafe pumps out smooth tunes, fresh fodder and mean espressos to a hip crowd of writers and indie fashionistas. Order a chèvre and walnut bagel, pull up a stool and start brainstorming that art-house masterpiece.

## A GOOD ROUTE

Hop on (and off) bus 4 for a cool trip around town.

Starting in Södermalm, slurp a smoothie at Hörnstull Mjölkbar (p100), before revamping the wardrobe and bookshelves at one of the impromptu flea markets or rummage sales that pop up at Hornstull Strand (p90) and off-beat bookshop Hallongrottan (p95). From Hornsgatan, catch a westbound bus 4 to Kungsholmen for killer sushi at Roppongi (p133), before travelling on to St Eriksplan for a mosey down Rörstrandsgatan (boxed text, p62) and fun foraging at Nostalgipalatset (p63). Hop off to admire Gunnar Asplund's Stadsbiblioteket (p57) before busing it to the end of the line in Östermalm. From here, it's a 25-minute stroll across Ladugårdsgärdet (Map pp110–11, G4) to sky-scraping Kaknästornet (p112) for sunset and skyline views. Pooped? Catch the 69 bus straight back into town.

### YU LOVE BIBIMBAB
*Korean*                                        €
☎ 644 39 90; Folkungagatan 89;
🕑 11.30am-2.30pm & 5-9pm Mon-Fri;
Ⓜ Medborgarplatsen
Believe it or not, the woman yelling orders at her husband was once a pop star in Korea. These days, she's a hit for her *bibimbab* (mixed rice), the only thing on the menu at her basic bolthole. Choose from chicken, beef, shrimp or vegetable – it's all bibimbab and it's all bibim-brilliant.

#  DRINK

In Östermalm, it's all about looking fab. In Södermalm, it's all about feeling fab, with friendlier crowds and a gung-ho party attitude. SoFo's Skånegatan is lined with hip hangouts, and you'll be hard pressed not to find a place that rocks your boat, whether it's a roaring beer hall or an arty Latin dive.

### AKKURAT *Beer Hall*
☎ 644 00 15; www.akkurat.se;
Hornsgatan 18; 🕑 11am-midnight Mon, 11am-1am Tue-Fri, 3pm-1am Sat, 6pm-1am Sun; Ⓜ Slussen
This down-to-earth drinking hole boasts 400 whiskys, a huge selection of Belgian ales and a good range of Swedish-made microbrews, notably the semi-divine Jämtlands Bryggeri trio Heaven, Hell and Fallen Angel. It has mus-

sels on the menu and free live R&B and rock on Sunday night.

### BARA VI *Bar*
☎ 669 58 55; www.baras.se in Swedish; Skånegatan 59; 🕑 5pm-1am Mon-Sat; Ⓜ Medborgarplatsen
Decked out in shagalicious floral wallpaper and plush red sofas, 'Just Us' is a popular hangout for trendy 30-somethings who like their drinks list long and smooth. Every second Wednesday from 8pm, Bara Unplugged (Skr30) sees local indie acts hit the stage. Scan www.baraunplugged.se (in Swedish) for the line-up.

### EL MUNDO *Bar & Art Gallery*
☎ 743 03 53; www.matkultur.nu in Swedish; Erstagatan 21; 🕑 5pm-midnight Mon-Thu & Sat, 4pm-midnight Fri; 🚌 2
Backgammon boards, Mexicana film posters and a bar made from pressed olive oil tins give this intimate hangout a sultry Latin vibe. There's art in the closet-sized backroom, a friendly 30-something crowd in the front room and an indie pop club night every other Wednesday. The last Saturday of the month is IDYLL; a pop-electro gay night.

### ERIKS GONDOLEN
*Restaurant & Cocktail Bar*
☎ 641 70 90; www.eriks.se; Stadsgården 6; 🕑 bar 11.30am-1am Mon-Fri,

NEIGHBOURHOODS

SÖDERMALM & LÅNGHOLMEN

4pm-1am Sat, restaurant 11.30am-2.30pm & 5pm-1am Mon-Fri, 4pm-1am Sat; Ⓜ Slussen
Perched atop Katarinahissen (p91), this place serves mean martinis and offers rooftop views. Slip into a leather armchair and play 'spot the landmark'. Respected chef Erik Lallerstedt runs the restaurant, matching the views with top-notch Swedish-Mediterranean food.

### Ⓨ KVARNEN
*Beer Hall & Nightclub*
☎ 643 03 80; www.kvarnen.com in Swedish; Tjärhovsgatan 4; ⏱ 11am-3am Mon-Fri, noon-3am Sat, 5pm-3am Sun; Ⓜ Medborgarplatsen
A cheerful mix of Hammarby football fans and Left Party former communists regularly packs Kvarnen, one of the best bars in Söder. The vast beer hall dates from 1907 and seeps tradition; beyond the scruffy old beerhounds and college boys, though, there are two slick bar-nightclubs – one red, one blue, both pumping. Queues are fairly constant but utterly justifiable.

### Ⓨ NADA *Bar*
☎ 644 70 20; Åsögatan 140; ⏱ 5pm-1am Mon-Sat; Ⓜ Medborgarplatsen
Forget Raymond. Everybody loves Nada. With its soft orange glow, mini chandelier and decadent

black-toned back bar, this cosy establishment pulls Söder's 20/30-something party people. Nightly, DJs play everything from alternative pop to '80s retro while the Raspberry Sour is the undisputed hit at the bar.

### Ⓨ PET SOUNDS BAR
*Restaurant, Bar & Nightclub*
☎ 643 82 25; www.petsoundsbar.se in Swedish; Skånegatan 80; ⏱ 5pm-1am Mon-Sat; Ⓜ Medborgarplatsen
While the restaurant does decent Italo-French dishes, the real fun happens downstairs in the glam-grunge basement, perpetually packed with indie die-hards, SoFo fashionistas and the odd Goth

Country in the city: the Tantolunden allotments

## COUNTRY CHILLING, SÖDER STYLE

For a soothing semibucolic interlude, take the Tunnelbana to Skanstull, walk past Eriks-dalsbadet and turn westward at the water's edge. Awaiting you is a wonderland of bob-bing boats and little wooden huts in picket-fenced allotments. Known as the Tantolunden allotments (Map pp88-9, C3), these tended vegetable patches were created during WWI to combat a shortage of potatoes and foodstuffs. Today, they're hot property for apart-ment-bound urbanites craving their own inner-city rural refuge.

rocker. Expect a mixed bag of live bands, release parties and kick-ass weekend DJs.

### ▼ RIVAL *Hotel Bar*
☎ 54 57 89 24; www.rival.se; Maria-torget 3; ⏲ 5pm-midnight Thu-Sat; Ⓜ Mariatorget
You'll find this sleek art deco number, complete with swish circular bar, inside designer hotel the Rival (co-owned by ABBA's Benny Andersson). While not Söder's top choice for atmos-pheric toasting, its architectural prowess merits a quick trip.

#  PLAY

### ☆ BIO RIO *Cinema*
☎ 669 95 00; www.biorio.se; Hornstull Strand 3; ⏲ 5-9pm Mon-Fri, 3-9pm Sat & Sun; Ⓜ Hornstull
The go-to theatre for all edgy new films, as well as special events like live opera performances or silent films accompanied by live music, Bio Rio anchors the Hornstull scene. The single-screen

cinema was built in the 1940s and includes a restaurant and cafe.

### ☆ DEBASER *Live Music*
☎ 462 98 60; www.debaser.se in Swedish; Karl Johanstorg 1, Slussen; ⏲ 7pm-1am, to 3am club nights Sun-Thu, 8pm-3am Fri & Sat; Ⓜ Slussen
Edgy, raw and tucked away under an overpass, this legendary rock club hosts live independent and bigger-name acts most nights. It also has a dance floor and wild club nights, including the ever-popular Club Killers, dedicated to ska and held on the last Wednes-day of every month. Sister club Debaser Medis rocks on at Med-borgarplatsen 8 (Map pp88–9).

### ☆ ERIKSDALSBADET *Swimming Pool*
☎ 50 84 02 58; Hammarby Slussväg 20; admission Skr75; ⏲ 6.30am-9pm Mon-Fri, 9am-5pm Sat & Sun; Ⓜ Skanstull
Stockholm's biggest swimming pool, Eriksdalsbadet has options for everyone: two lap pools, jacuzzis, waterslides, a children's

play area, wave machines, sauna, steam room and an outdoor pool. There's also a gym and sunbeds, if you're feeling self-conscious about your bikini.

### ⭐ FOLKOPERAN *Opera*
☎ 616 07 50; www.folkoperan.se; Hornsgatan 72; tickets Skr250-380; ☾ varies; Ⓜ Zinkensdamm

Immensely popular and internationally renowned, Folkoperan gives opera a thoroughly modern overhaul with its intimate, cutting-edge and sometimes controversial productions of both classic and contemporary works. Book weeks ahead as seats sell out quickly. Check the website for booking details.

### ⭐ LADY PATRICIA
*Nightclub & Restaurant*
☎ 743 05 70; www.patricia.st; Stadsgårdskajen 152; admission Skr80; ☾ 6pm-3am Sun; Ⓜ Slussen

Half-price seafood, nonstop *schlager* music and decks packed with sexy Swedes and drag queens make this former royal yacht a gay Sunday night ritual. Kick off at the legendary restaurant (book a month in advance), then head to the upper dance floor where lager-happy punters sing along to Swedish Eurovision entries with a bemusing lack of irony.

### ⭐ LILJEHOLMSBADET
*Swimming Pool*
☎ 668 67 80; Bergsunds Strand 2; adult/under 7yr/7-19yr/concession Skr60/free/20/40; ☾ 7am-7pm Mon women only, 7am-7pm Fri men only, 7am-4pm Tue & Wed, 7am-5pm Thu, 8am-2pm Sat; Ⓜ Hornstull

Housed inside a floating wooden pontoon on Lake Mälaren, this quaint little 1930s pool and sauna is a heart-stealer. Single-sex swimming days encourage Scandi-style skinny-dipping while the occasional live jazz and classical concert will add swing to your swim.

### ⭐ MARIE LAVEAU
*Live Music & Nightclub*
☎ 668 85 00; www.marielaveau.se; Hornsgatan 66; ☾ 5pm-midnight Mon-Wed, 5pm-3am Thu-Sat; Ⓜ Mariatorget

Housed in a former sausage factory, this kicking Söder playpen draws boho-chic hedonists who like to party till (relatively) late. While the grunge-chic bar and restaurant serves killer cocktails and fusion food, the sweaty downstairs club keeps punters grinding to live bands or hot-name DJs from Stockholm to Noo Yoik.

### ⭐ MOSEBACKE ETABLISSEMENT
*Bar, Live Music, Nightclub & Culture*
☎ 55 60 98 90; www.mosebacke.se; Mosebacketorg 3; admission Skr50-100;

## THE CLIFFS OF SÖDER

For some of the best views over Stockholm, it's hard to beat the northern cliffs of Södermalm. From Slussen (Map pp88–9, F2), Katarinavägen heads east above the Södermalm shore towards the quaint old street of Fjällgatan. Along the way, soak up stunning views over fabled Gamla Stan and turreted Östermalm and towards the inner archipelago. To the west of Slussen, the lush, leafy path of Monteliusvägen (Map pp88–9, E2) offers gob-smacking views of the city with a side-serve of picture-perfect cottages and picket-fenced gardens.

☽ 5pm-1am Mon-Thu, 5pm-2am Fri, 10.30am-2am Sat, 10.30am-1am Sun; Ⓜ Slussen

This multifunction party palace is a thumping institution. August Strindberg once hung out here, the lofty terrace is a summer-night must, and the club nights are among the city's best – don't miss veteran Friday favourite Blacknuss, with its gospel/soul/R&B tunes. Theatre and cabaret also make the occasional splash, while regular live-music jams span from Aussie rock to Nordic indie pop.

### ☆ SÖDRA TEATERN
*Bar, Live Music, Nightclub & Culture*
☎ 55 69 72 30; www.sodrateatern.com; Mosebacketorg 1-3; admission varies; ☽ 7pm-1am Thu, 7pm-2am Fri & Sat, summer bar 5pm-1am Tue-Thu, 5pm-2am Fri & Sat, 3pm-1am Sun; Ⓜ Slussen

If it's fiery flamenco, gypsy wedding tunes or Muslim stand-up comedy from London you're after, chances are you'll find it at this cultural hothouse, complete with lush La Scala–style theatre. Check the website for upcoming events, which range from live world music to erudite debates and the monthly exotica of club night Re:Orient.

# >ÖSTERMALM, GÄRDET & LADUGÅRDSGÄRDET

Home to the rich, the famous and the fastidious, Östermalm is Stockholm's spangly party hotspot. At its heart is Stureplan, a bustling plaza marked by an odd-mod pavilion dubbed 'Svampen' (the mushroom). It's here that the fashion-fabulous meet before hitting the A-list hangouts, like Riche, Nox and Laroy, for late-night champagne and celebrity attitude.

During the day you'll find them scouring *fin de siècle* streets like Grev Turegatan, Humlegårdsgatan, Linnégatan and Sibyllegatan for catwalk couture, rare Italian perfumes and classic Scandinavian design. Hedonism aside, this former city marshland harbours a few cultural gems,

## ÖSTERMALM, GÄRDET & LADUGÅRDSGÄRDET

Please see over for map

including the Armémuseum and Greta Garbo's former stomping ground, Kungliga Dramatiska Teatern.

Bordering the water's edge at its southern end is Stockholm's grandest boulevard, Strandvägen, a haughty mix of turreted buildings, docked yachts and perfect twilight ambling. To the northeast, the residential district of Gärdet sits close to one of Stockholm's sharpest contemporary art galleries, the portside Magasin 3. Directly east of Östermalm, the vast open parkland of Ladugårdsgärdet sprawls westward like a giant green carpet sprinkled with love-struck couples, Scandilicious joggers and the iconic Kaknästornet, a soaring retro TV tower-cum-observation deck with sterling Stockholm views.

#  SEE

## ARMÉMUSEUM

☎ 51 95 63 00; www.armemuseum
.se; Riddargatan 13; adult/under
19yr Skr40/free, Stockholm Card free;
🕑 11am-8pm Tue, 11am-5pm Wed-Sun
Sep-Jun, 10am-8pm Tue, 10am-5pm
Wed-Mon Jul & Aug; Ⓜ Östermalmstorg; ♿

Take a walk on the dark side of human nature at the Royal Army Museum, where three levels of engrossing exhibitions explore the horrors of war through art, weaponry and life-size reconstructions of charging horsemen, forlorn barracks and starving civilians. For a taste of medieval torture, hop on the replica 'sawhorse'.

## ETNOGRAFISKA MUSEET

☎ 51 95 50 00; www.etnografiska.se;
Djurgårdsbrunnsvägen 34; adult/under
21yr Skr60/free, Stockholm Card free;
🕑 10am-5pm Tue-Fri, 11am-5pm Sat &
Sun; 🚌 69; ♿

Next door to the Tekniska Museet (p113), the National Museum of Ethnography focuses on non-European cultures. Highly original temporary exhibitions (ranging from Amazon photography to the macabre etchings of Mexican artist José Guadalupe Posada) complement permanent collection highlights like Mali crocodile masks, Mongolian temple tents and a Japanese teahouse. The formerly in-house restaurant **Babajan** ( 🕑 5-11pm Mon-Sat, 1-7pm Sun), serving a stellar Afro-Asian-Middle Eastern menu, has moved to Katarina Banggata 75.

## HISTORISKA MUSEET

☎ 51 95 56 00; www.historiska.se;
Narvavägen 13-17; adult/under 19yr/con-
cession Skr60/free/40, Stockholm Card
free; 🕑 11am-5pm Tue-Sun, to 8pm
Thu Oct-Apr, 10am-5pm daily May-Sep;
Ⓜ Karlaplan; ♿

From Iron Age ice-skates to Renaissance triptychs, Sweden's prime

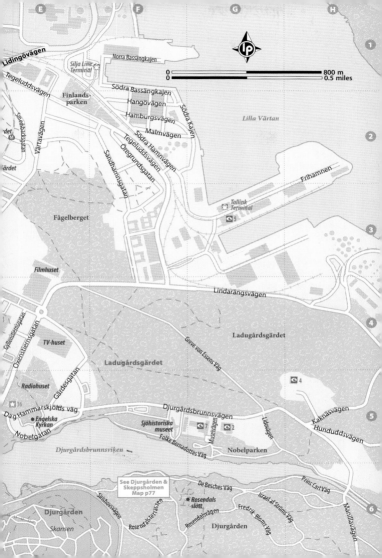

historical collection spans nearly 14,000 years of Swedish history and culture. The undisputed highlight is the subterranean Gold Room, a brooding chamber gleaming with Viking bling and rare historical jewels. The most astonishing artefact is the 5th-century, seven-ringed gold collar with 458 carved figures, which weighs 823g. Found in Västergötland in the 19th century, it was probably used by pagan priests in ritualistic ceremonies. To use the museum's fantastic free digital audio guides, bring some ID.

16yr Skr30/free/15, Stockholm Card free; ⏰ 10am-5pm Mon-Wed, 10am-9pm Thu-Sat, 10am-6pm Sun Jan-Apr, 9am-10pm daily May-Aug, 10am-9pm Mon-Sat, 10am-5pm Sun Sep-Dec; 🚌 69
The dowdy retro decor atop this 155m-high communications tower – Stockholm's tallest building – is thoroughly compensated by the 360-degree views over Stockholm and the lush green archipelago. Skip the restaurant for the cafe, where a mean chocolate cake makes the perfect prop for ferry-spotting and sunset vistas.

### 🄲 KAKNÄSTORNET
☎ 667 21 05; www.kaknastornet.se; Ladugårdsgärdet; adult/under 7yr/under

### 🄲 MAGASIN 3
☎ 54 56 80 40; www.magasin3.com; elevator 4, Magasin 3 Bldg, Frihamnen;

Walk on the dark side at the Armémuseum (p109)

adult/under 20yr/concession Skr40/free/30; ⏰ 11am-7pm Thu, 11am-5pm Fri-Sun during exhibitions; 🚌 76; ♿ Aptly set in a gritty dockside warehouse, Magasin 3 is one of Stockholm's brat-pack galleries. Its six to eight annual shows of contemporary art often feature specially commissioned, site-specific work from names like Siobhán Hapaska, James Turrell, Ronald Jones, Katharina Grosse and provocative American artist Paul McCarthy.

### 📷 ÖSTERMALMS SALUHALL

www.saluhallen.com; Östermalmstorg; admission free; ⏰ 9.30am-6pm Mon-Thu, 9.30am-6.30pm Fri, 9.30am-4pm Sat, to 2pm Sat July; Ⓜ Östermalmstorg; ♿ Stockholm's market diva, Östermalms Saluhall (p15) is a must-see mix of 1880s architecture, heady aromas, gorgeous stalls and old-fashioned neighbourly hobnobbing. Lust over lobsters, pig out on salmon pudding and get the lowdown on Swedish gourmet from the veteran market vendors.

### 📷 TEKNISKA MUSEET

☎ 450 56 00; www.tekniskamuseet.se; Museivägen 7; adult/under 6yr/6-19yr/senior Skr70/free/30/40, Stockholm Card free; ⏰ 10am-5pm Mon-Fri, to 8pm Wed, 11am-5pm Sat & Sun; 🚌 69; ♿ The biggest drawcard at the vast and vibrant Museum of Sci-

ence and Technology is CINO4, Sweden's first 4-D cinema. Once you've been shaken, stirred and possibly squirted, check out the rest of this dazzling multimedia complex, which includes chatty Japanese robots, Sweden's first motor car (from 1897), an artificial mine, a retro telephone collection and the Teknorama Science Centre, with its interactive displays on topics such as the basic principles of physics.

# SHOP

From denim to dining chairs, if you bag it in this part of town, chances are it's highly designed and highly priced. Shop here for cult Scandinavian furniture and fabrics and super-cool threads from Stockholm and beyond.

### Lina
*Bartender at Story Hotel bar in Östermalm (www.storyhotel.com)*

**Where are some nice places in Stockholm to go for a drink?** Here! This is nice actually. Later it gets really lively with lots of music and a fun crowd. Nada (p104) has good music and a nice crowd. There are good bars all along that street (Åsögatan). **What other places do people go?** I usually go out in the south, in Södermalm. It's cheap! I used to go there a lot when I was younger. Each place has its own generation who go there.

### ANNA HOLTBLAD *Fashion*
☎ 54 50 22 20; www.annaholtblad.com; Grev Turegatan 13; ⏲ 10.30am-6.30pm Mon-Fri, 10.30am-4pm Sat; Ⓜ Östermalmstorg

Stylish but never faddish, Anna Holtblad is famed for her earthy women's knits, classic-cut coats and contemporary twists on folkloric designs. The shop itself was designed by Thomas Sandell, one of Sweden's stellar architects and interior designers.

### ASPLUND *Design*
☎ 662 52 84; Sibyllegatan 31; ⏲ 11am-6pm Mon-Fri year-round, 11am-2pm Sat summer; Ⓜ Östermalmstorg

This showroom for the hip furniture maker stocks its own designs as well as carpets and accessories from internationally known brands like Bruno Mathsson and de Nord. Like a high-end IKEA, it's a perfect place to indulge in aspirational browsing.

### BIRGER JARLSPASSAGEN *Fashion*
Birger Jarlsgatan 9; Ⓜ Östermalmstorg

Designed by architect Ludvig Peterson, this fetching *fin de siècle* arcade contains a number of stylish gems. **Mrs H** ( ☎ 678 02 00; www.mrsh.se; ⏲ 11am-6.30pm Mon-Fri, noon-4pm Sat) is a fashionista staple, famed for its savvy collection of cosmetics, vintage boots and top-notch denim labels Citizens of Humanity and Sass & Bide. Indulge your lust for exotic and decadent underthings at **Agent Provocateur** ( ☎ 678 28 20; ⏲ 10.30am-6.30pm Mon-Fri, 11am-5pm Sat), or feast your greedy eyes upon the knockout gems at a branch of former pop star Efva Attling's avant-garde **jewellery shop** ( ☎ 611 90 80; ⏲ 10.30am-6pm Mon-Fri, 11am-4pm Sat).

### BLUEBERRY *Health*
☎ 661 25 50; www.blueberrylifestyle .se in Swedish; Sibyllegatan 15; ⏲ 10am-7pm Mon-Thu, 10am-6pm Fri, 11am-3pm Sat; Ⓜ Östermalmstorg

Health gets haute at this uberhip wholefoods shop, complete with tiny tea bar and trendy buys like soya candles, biodegradable yoga mats and designer paternity bags (as worn by Brad Pitt). With healthy hunks on your mind, grab yourself a fresh Love smoothie (chocolate, cardamom and pear) and *prêt-à-manger* lunch pack from the health bar out the back.

### FILIPPA K *Fashion*
☎ 54 58 88 88; www.filippak.com; Grev Turegatan 18; ⏲ 11am-7pm Mon-Fri, 11am-5pm Sat, noon-4pm Sun; Ⓜ Östermalmstorg

Filippa K is the epitome of regulation Nordic style – think sleek looks, classic cuts and sensible sombre tones. The store, a minimalist masterpiece designed by

AARO Arkitekter, also stocks shoes, accessories and perfect books for your coffee table.

### HEDENGRENS *Books*
☎ 611 51 32; Sturegallerian; ⏱ 10am-7pm Mon-Fri, 10am-6pm Sat, noon-5pm Sun; Ⓜ Östermalmstorg

This surprisingly capacious bookstore inside Sturegallerian has possibly Stockholm's largest selection of books in English; go downstairs and try not to get dizzy browsing the shelves in the store's circular layout.

### J LINDEBERG *Fashion*
☎ 678 61 65; www.jlindeberg.com; Grev Turegatan 7; ⏱ 10am-7pm Mon-Fri, 10am-6pm Sat, noon-5pm Sun; Ⓜ Östermalmstorg

Like neighbouring Filippa K, J Lindeberg is a Swedish fashion staple and a long-time hit with PR and media types. Expect classic chic with irreverent twists. The store also stocks the street-wise JL Future Sports and JL Golf lines.

### MODERNITY *Design*
☎ 20 80 25; www.modernity.se; Sibyllegatan 6; ⏱ noon-6pm Mon-Fri, 11am-3pm Sat; Ⓜ Östermalmstorg

A bit like a museum where you can take home the booty, world-famous Modernity stocks cult furniture from 20th-century Scandinavian greats like Alvar Aalto,

Josef Frank, Arne Jacobsen and Bruno Mathsson, as well as iconic glassware, lighting and jewellery. Best of all, Scottish owner Andrew Duncanson doesn't mind a natter about his stock – sale or not.

### NORDISKA GALLERIET *Design*
☎ 442 83 60; www.nordiskagalleriet.se in Swedish; Nybrogatan 11; ⏱ 10am-6pm Mon-Fri, noon-4pm Sat & Sun; Ⓜ Östermalmstorg

This sprawling showroom is a design freak's El Dorado – think Hannes Wettstein chairs, Hella Jongerius sofas, Alvar Aalto vases and mini-sized Verner Panton chairs for style-sensitive kids. Luggage-friendly options include designer coat-hangers, erudite architecture books and bright Marimekko paper napkins for uberstylish wiping.

### PEAK PERFORMANCE *Fashion*
☎ 611 34 00; Biblioteksgatan 18; www.peakperformance.com; ⏱ 10am-7pm Mon-Fri, 10am-5pm Sat, noon-5pm Sun; Ⓜ Östermalmstorg

Snow bunnies of both sexes head here for svelte and stylish tough-weather threads and accessories. Established in the ski town of Åre, this is the place for a high-tech snow jacket or sexy sweater for an evening at the chalet.

### 🏠 RÖNNELLS ANTIKVARIAT
*Secondhand Books*

☎ 54 50 15 60; www.ronnells.se; Birger Jarlsgatan 32; ⏰ 10am-6pm Mon-Fri, 11am-3pm Sat; Ⓜ Östermalmstorg

From vintage Astrid Lindgren books to dusty 19th-century travel guides, the 100,000-strong collection of books here, many in English, make this one of the meatiest secondhand bookshops in town. Forage through the sales rack for a new dog-eared friend.

### 🏠 SIBYLLANS KAFFE & TEHANDEL *Coffee & Tea*

☎ 662 06 63; Sibyllegatan 35; ⏰ 10am-6pm Mon-Fri; Ⓜ Östermalmstorg

Looking venerable with its sombre wooden interior and rows of giant tea tins, this tea and coffee peddler has been filling pots and plungers since WWI. Try the house blend of mixed green teas or go Latin with a Bialetti cafeteria and a block of Columbian-bean chocolate.

### 🏠 SPRALL
*Children's Clothes & Toys*

☎ 662 31 30; www.sprall.se; Sibyllegatan 18; ⏰ 10.30am-6pm Mon-Fri, 11am-3pm Sat; Ⓜ Östermalmstorg

Sprall spoils the little ones with super-cute designer clothes from Stockholm and across the world (the mini-kimono tops from New York designer Lucky Wang will leave you ga-ga). Mix and match with top-notch wooden toys, knitted teddies and Mr and Mrs Baker dolls. There's another branch inside NK (p62).

### 🏠 SVENSKT TENN *Design*

☎ 670 16 00; www.svenskttenn.se; Strandvägen 5; ⏰ 10am-6pm Mon-Fri, 10am-4pm Sat, noon-4pm Sun; Ⓜ Östermalmstorg

This legendary design store was once the stomping ground of Josef Frank, whose modernist furniture and floral-patterned fabrics are now the stuff of Swedish design legend. Nab some of his cult printed fabrics, or simply go for the top-notch lighting, homewares

Svenskt Tenn's fab floral fabrics

ÖSTERMALM, GÄRDET & LADUGÅRDSGÄRDET

and furniture from Swedish design heavyweights.

 # EAT

From clean-lined Scandi classics to faux-French bistros, Östermalm's obsession with style extends to the table. The common theme here is 'see and be seen', so slick up, sit by the window and toast with top-shelf bubbly.

### 🍴 CAFÉ SATURNUS Cafe €

☎ 611 77 00; Eriksbergsgatan 6;
🕙 8am-8pm Mon-Thu, 8am-7pm Fri, 10am-7pm Sat & Sun; Ⓜ Östermalmstorg

Everyone from yummy mummies to peckish princesses flock here for Gallic-inspired baguettes, pastries and creamy *café au lait*. While Saturnus' claim that it was the first to introduce Stockholm to 'proper' coffee is hotly contested, there's little doubt that its *kanelbullar* (cinnamon bun) is the

city's biggest…and dare we say its best.

### 🍴 EAST Asian Fusion €€€

☎ 611 49 59; www.east.se; Stureplan 13; 🕙 restaurant 11.30am-1am Mon-Fri, 5pm-1am Sat & Sun, bar 11.30am-3am Mon-Fri, 5pm-3am Sat & Sun; Ⓜ Östermalmstorg

It was East that snapped Stockholm out of its lemon-chicken fixation. Years on, this eternally hip resto-bar still pulls in the punters for perfect Asian grub in Scandi-Jap surrounds. While the bar skills are patchy, the chefs, DJs and swimming piranhas will keep you snapping those chopsticks happily.

### 🍴 ELVERKET International €€

☎ 661 25 62; www.restaurangelverket .se; Linnégatan 69; 🕙 lunch 11am-2pm Mon-Fri, dinner 5-11pm Tue-Sat, brunch 11am-3pm Sat, 11am-4pm Sun; Ⓜ Karlaplan

---

### WORTH THE TRIP

The former home and studio of master sculptor Carl Milles, **Millesgården** ( ☎ 446 75 90; www.millesgarden.se in Swedish; Carl Milles Väg 2, Lidingö; adult/under 18yr/concession Skr80/free/60, Stockholm Card free; 🕙 noon-5pm Tue-Sun Oct–mid-May, 11am-5pm daily mid-May–Sep; Ⓜ Ropsten, then bus 207 direct or bus 202, 204, 205, 206, 212 to Torsvik plus 5min walk) is a Stockholm high point, both literally and figuratively. Sculpture, gardens and glittering vistas aside, Millesgården is also the place to catch a glimpse of the organ reputedly played by Mozart's father, as well as art attributed to the likes of Canaletto, Donatello and Clouet.

For the complete lowdown on the buildings and the collections, grab a copy of the detailed catalogue and map (Skr15) at the front desk. See also p19.

Best for a lazy weekend brunch, slick and cosy Elverket sits in an old electricity plant, alongside Kungliga Dramatiska Teatern's more experimental stage (see p123). Here, a mix of Capote-styled intellectuals, gossipy girlfriends and designer dads nurse hangovers over Scandi staples, Asian extras and sinfully good chocolate brownies.

### 🍴 HALV GREK PLUS TURK
*Greek/Turkish* €€€
☎ 665 94 22; www.halvgrekplusturk.se; Jungfrugatan 33; 🕑 5.30pm-midnight; Ⓜ Stadion

Majolica tiles and mosque-inspired lighting accompany the moreish *meze* at this cosy Stockholm staple. Three *meze* dishes per person should suffice, with must-tries including basil-fried halloumi cheese with walnut and plum chutney, honey and fennel blackened chicken wings, and sesame-glazed star anise and cinnamon-braised red pork.

### 🍴 LISA ELMQVIST
*Seafood* €€€
☎ 55 34 04 10; www.lisaelmqvist.se; Östermalms Saluhall, Östermalmstorg; 🕑 9.30am-6pm Mon-Thu, 9.30am-6.30pm Fri, 9.30am-4pm Sat, to 2pm Jul; Ⓜ Östermalmstorg

Seafood fans, look no further. This Stockholm legend, suitably snug inside historic Östermalms

Saluhall (p113), is never short of a satisfied lunchtime crowd. The menu changes daily, so let the waiters order for you; whether it's lobster pancakes or seared Sichuan pepper char fillets, you won't be disappointed. In the warmer months, sup in the sun at sister bistro **Lisa på Torget** ( ☎ 55 34 04 50; 🕑 noon-11pm), slap bang on the square outside.

### 🍴 SABAI-SOONG *Thai* €€
☎ 663 12 77; www.sabai.se in Swedish; Linnégatan 39B; 🕑 4.30-10pm Mon, to 11pm Tue-Thu, to midnight Fri, 4pm-midnight Sat, 4-10pm Sun; Ⓜ Östermalmstorg

Super-kitsch Sabai-Soong is keeping it real despite the snooty address. A hit with families and fashionistas alike, its tropical-trash Day-Glo interior is the perfect place to chow down on simple and faithful versions of *tod man pla* and fiery green curry.

### 🍴 STUREHOF *Swedish* €€€
☎ 440 57 30; www.sturehof.com; Stureplan 2; 🕑 11am-2am Mon-Fri, noon-2am Sat, 1pm-2am Sun (kitchen closes 1am); Ⓜ Östermalmstorg

An empty table is just as rare as a mediocre meal at this crisp, Jonas Bohlin–designed brasserie. Slap bang on Stureplan, Sturehof is the perfect place to enjoy seafood, champagne sessions

**WORTH THE TRIP**

Perched on the edge of the Stockholm archipelago and overlooking the sea, **Yasuragi** ( ☎ 747 64 00; www.yasuragi.se; Hamndalsvägen 6, Saltsjö-Boo; day spa/meal packages from Skr800; ⏰ 8am-10pm; Vaxholm ferry from Strömkajen to Hasseludden jetty or bus 444 to Orminge Centrum then bus 417 to Hamndalsvägen plus 10min walk) is Sweden's first Japanese spa.

Appropriately minimalist in a Scandi-Jap style, the resort features a luxe indoor pool, indoor and outdoor hot spring Jacuzzis (so you can soak in the snow), heavenly treatments (try a floating massage) and courses ranging from Zen meditation to sushi-making.

The in-house **teppanyaki restaurant** ( ☎ 747 64 63; ⏰ lunch 11.30am-2pm, dinner 6pm-midnight) is Stockholm's finest and the hotel rooms (choose from ryokan or Scandi-chic) mean you don't have to leave in a hurry. Book treatments and accommodation in advance.

and gratuitous people-watching. Full and fulfilled, pop into tiny Obaren (opposite) for a post-meal martini.

### 🍴 STUREKATTEN Cafe     €

☎ 611 16 12; Riddargatan 4; ⏰ 8am-8pm Mon-Fri, 9am-6pm Sat, 11am-6pm Sun; Ⓜ Östermalmstorg

Looking like a life-sized doll's house, this vintage cafe is a fetching blend of antique chairs, oil paintings, ladies who lunch and waitresses in black-and-white garb. Slip into a salon chair, pour some tea and nibble on the must-try apple pies and cinnamon scrolls.

### 🍴 VASSA EGGEN
New Swedish     €€€

☎ 21 61 69; www.vassaeggen.com; Birger Jarlsgatan 29; ⏰ lunch 11.30am-

2pm Mon-Fri, dinner 6-10pm Mon, 6-11pm Tue-Sat; Ⓜ Östermalmstorg

Featuring a domed dining room sitting beyond a glassed birch forest, this stylish dining pad is named after Somerset Maugham's novel *The Razor's Edge*. With sharply executed dishes like oxtail tortellini with mascarpone cheese and a long and luscious wine list, it all makes perfect sense. Book ahead.

# 🍸 DRINK

You should dress up to drink in this part of town, where fashion sense is as crucial as a well-mixed margarita.

### 🍸 BRASSERIE GODOT
Restaurant & Bar

☎ 660 06 14; www.godot.se; Grev Turegatan 36; ⏰ 5pm-1am Mon-Sat; Ⓜ Östermalmstorg

Pop in to see the giant murals by graphic artist Erik Eriksson, then work your way through one of Stockholm's finest cocktail menus. Unsurprisingly popular is the John Holmes, a long drink with plenty of kink. Thursday nights are best with a vibrant vibe and room to move.

### ☒ HOTELLET *Restaurant & Bar*
☎ 442 89 00; www.hotellet.info; Linnégatan 18; ⏲ 5pm-midnight Mon & Tue, 5pm-1am Wed & Thu, 4pm-1am Fri, 6pm-1am Sat; Ⓜ Östermalmstorg

Named for the hotel it never became, this split-level hotspot is home to blonde bombshells, impish brunettes and trendy studs with photo-shoot hair. There's even a trés-chic garden by architect outfit NOD. Not surprisingly, the place has had its fair share of style mag coverage, which seems perfectly justified when sipping apple martinis next to the yummy Nordic eye Scandi.

### ☒ NOX *Restaurant & Bar*
☎ 54 58 24 00; www.nox.se in Swedish; Grev Turegatan 30; ⏲ 5pm-1am Tue-Fri, 6pm-1am Sat; Ⓜ Östermalmstorg

Stockholm's style council can't get enough of the designer back terrace here, with its mood lighting, snug poufs and chi-chi wooden decking. Inside, leather lounges, a luminous green bar (try a frozen champagne daiquiri), and smooth DJ sessions Thursday to Saturday keep the party people purring.

### ☒ OBAREN *Bar*
☎ 440 57 30; www.sturehof.com; Stureplan 2; ⏲ 7pm-2am Sat-Thu, 5pm-2am Fri; Ⓜ Östermalm

This bar deep inside Sturehof restaurant is a popular late-night, last-call stop; it's less manic at other times, and a cool place to hang out. The standing-room-only bar at the front of Sturehof is a popular

Waiting for...cocktails at Brasserie Godot

after-work rendezvous and the perfect place to flaunt those new House of Dagmar threads.

### Y RICHE *Restaurant & Bar*
☎ 54 50 35 60; www.riche.se; Birger Jarlsgatan 4; ⏰ 11.30am-2am Tue-Fri, 5pm-2am Sat; Ⓜ Östermalmstorg
While both bars here are hugely popular, the smaller Lilla Riche is the current choice of Östermalm's hip parade. Buffed bartenders mix the drinks, skilled DJs mix the music and a tightly packed crowd of media types and celebrities flirt, flaunt and step on each other's manicured toes. The adjoining **Riche restaurant** ( ⏰ 11.30am-midnight Mon, 11.30am-1am Tue, 11.30am-2am Wed-Fri, noon-2am Sat) is one of Stockholm's best for Swedish-Mediterranean cuisine.

### Y SCANDIC ANGLAIS
*Hotel Bar*
☎ 51 73 40 00; www.scandic-hotels .com; Humlegårdsgatan 23; ⏰ 10am-2am, alcohol served from 11.30am Mon-Fri, 10am-2am, alcohol served from noon Sat & Sun; Ⓜ Östermalmstorg
This swank hotel bar, just a quick hop north of Stureplan, has a wide-open layout that makes it equally inviting for after-work drinks or midday coffee breaks – belly up to the bar or find a quiet corner for a business chat. Late nights, the space fills up with the cocktail crowd.

### Y VIOLA *Restaurant & Bar*
☎ 664 55 35; info@restaurangviola.se; Humlegårdsgatan 14; ⏰ 5pm-midnight Mon-Wed, 5pm-1am Thu & Fri, 6pm-1am Sat; Ⓜ Östermalmstorg
Chic and just a little camp, Viola is a chi-chi combination of champagne leather booths, mini chandeliers and flouncy floral wallpaper. Glam up and join the gorgeous for perfect cocktails and a healthy round of air kissing.

## ⭐ PLAY
High-flying Östermalm loves a little *dolce vita*, from opulent theatre and symphonies to decadent thermal soaking. Its Stureplan district is also home to Stockholm's glitziest dance clubs, where door bitches rule the roost and where beauty comes from without. Love it or loathe it, this is where you'll find most of the late-night parties, so style up and don't look too eager to get through the doors.

### ✪ BERWALDHALLEN
*Concert Hall*
☎ 784 18 00; www.sr.se/berwaldhallen; Dag Hammarskjölds väg 3; tickets Skr65-500; ⏰ box office noon-6pm Mon-Fri, closed Jul; 🚌 69
Named after the Swedish composer Franz Berwald, this

## WORTH THE TRIP

Upstaging Östermalm in the real-estate stakes, 17th-century royal palace **Ulriksdals Slottet** ( ☎ 402 61 30; www.kungahuset.se; adult/under 7yr/7-19yr incl Orangery Museum Skr70/free/35; ⏰ guided tours only noon, 1pm, 2pm, 3pm Tue-Sun Jun-Aug; Ⓜ Bergshamra, then bus 540) sprawls waterside in uberlush Ulriksdals Park. This was home to King Gustav VI Adolf until 1973. The living room boasts one of the finest 20th-century interiors in Sweden, while the drawing room houses furniture designed by Carl Malmsten. The highly civilised **Orangery** ( ⏰ noon-4pm Tue-Sun Jun-Aug) contains 18th- and 19th-century Swedish sculpture while summer music and ballet concerts usually take place in the **Confidencen** ( ☎ 85 70 16; www.confidencen.se in Swedish), Sweden's oldest rococo theatre. Check the website for festival dates or contact the tourist office (p184).

late-1970s concert hall is at the top of its game, despite being mostly underground. It's home to the Swedish Radio Symphony Orchestra and world-renowned Radiokören (Swedish Radio Choir), and it also hosts the annual August Baltic Sea Festival, a classical music extravaganza featuring orchestras, choirs and soloists from several Baltic countries, including Russia.

### ⭐ BIOGRAFEN STURE Cinema
☎ 678 85 48; www.biosture.se in Swedish; Birger Jarlsgatan 41; Ⓜ Östermalmstorg
It mightn't have the vintage charm of the Zita down the road, but at least you'll find a flick in English. The leaning is art house, and the Baby-bio screenings mean bubs can waaaaah to their hearts' content.

### ⭐ COCKTAIL CLUB @ GRODAN GREV TURE Bar & Nightclub
☎ 679 61 00; www.grodan.se; Grev Turegatan 16; admission Skr80-150; ⏰ 10pm-3am Fri & Sat, occasionally open Thu; Ⓜ Östermalmstorg
Hiding somewhat incongruously below a mock-baroque dining salon is one of Stockholm's best party spots, Cocktail Club. Expect A-list DJ talent from Stockholm to London and Berlin (including Ben Watt, Alan Braxe and Eric Prydz), all working the wax and pumping out house and electro for Stockholm's sweat-soaked club kids.

### ⭐ KUNGLIGA DRAMATISKA TEATERN Theatre
☎ 667 06 80; www.dramaten.se in Swedish; Nybroplan; tickets Skr120-300; ⏰ box office noon-7pm Tue-Sat, noon-4pm Sun; Ⓜ Östermalmstorg

NEIGHBOURHOODS

ÖSTERMALM, GÄRDET & LADUGÅRDSGÄRDET

The Royal Dramatic Theatre (Dramaten) is the grand dame of the Swedish stage, with productions ranging from Shakespeare to Strindberg in a lavish art nouveau setting. This is chez Bergman, where the famous director has been a driving force since the 1960s. Dramaten's experimental stage, **Elverket** (Linnégatan 69; same contact details), pushes the boundaries with an edgier program performed in a converted power station. Ticket discounts include 10% for seniors, 35% for students and 50% for those under 25.

### ⭐ LAROY
*Restaurant, Bar & Nightclub*
☎ 54 50 37 00; Birger Jarlsgatan 20; admission Skr100; ⏰ 10pm-3am Wed, Fri & Sat; Ⓜ Östermalmstorg

This Stureplan 'it kid' draws the young and the beautiful for self-conscious cocktail sessions. Start off the night with French-fusion food in the restaurant, before trying your luck at charming the catwalk-worthy crowd. Tip: contact the venue five days ahead to get your name on the door.

### ⭐ SOLIDARITET *Nightclub*
☎ 678 10 50; www.solidaritetstureplan .se; Lästmakargatan 3; ⏰ 10pm-5am Wed-Sat; Ⓜ Östermalmstorg

If you're into house tunes, here's your new hangout. Some of the

**TREADING THE BOARDS**

Designed by architect Fredrik Liljekvist and completed in 1908, the oh-so-opulent Kungliga Dramatiska Teatern (p123) is an architectural treasure trove, featuring exterior sculpture by Carl Milles and Theodor Lundberg, and a foyer ceiling painted by Carl Larsson.

If you can't get seats to a show, join a one-hour guided tour of the theatre (Skr50), conducted in English at 3pm on Monday to Saturday, mid-June to mid-August.

scene's biggest names have manned the decks here, from Sweden's Stonebridge, Sebastian Ingrosso, Axwell and Steve Angello to imports like Amsterdam's DJ Santito of Sorobon party fame. The queues are long and the bouncers are picky. Good luck.

### ⭐ SPY BAR *Nightclub*
☎ 54 50 76 55; www.thespybar.com; Birger Jarlsgatan 20; admission Skr90-125; ⏰ 10pm-5am Wed-Sat; Ⓜ Östermalmstorg

The former ice-queen of the club scene has reinvented itself. Gone are the reality-TV brats and stuck-up staff, and in their place is a mock-baroque look and chilled-out combo of media types and indie fashionistas for whom well-mixed drinks and smooth electro tunes matter more than Prada mules and sports cars. It's not as cool as it used to be, and that's a good thing.

## ⭐ STUREBADET *Spa*
☎ 54 50 15 00; www.sturebadet.se; Sturegallerian 36, Stureplan; day pass Skr495-595, minimum age 18yr; ⏱ 6.30am-10pm Mon-Fri, 9am-7pm Sat & Sun; Ⓜ Östermalmstorg

Old Norse meets Ottoman chic at Stockholm's poshest pool, gym and spa, once the haunt of Greta Garbo and still a favourite with the rich and famously frazzled. For full-on Scandi bliss, try the Samezen treatment (Skr1590, 80 minutes), choreographed to Sami *jojk* music and performed in a tepee-inspired room. While day passes are readily available, treatments should be booked two weeks in advance.

## ⭐ STURECOMPAGNIET
*Nightclub*
☎ 54 50 76 70; www.sturecompagniet.se; Stureplan 4; admission Skr120; ⏱ 10pm-3am Thu-Sat; Ⓜ Östermalmstorg

Swedish soap stars, '80s-inspired glitz, and look-at-me attitude set the scene at this sprawling party playpen. Dress like the Beckhams, (try to) charm the bouncers, and slip your way oh-so-subtly into the VIP room to the left of the entrance for ab-fab antics.

NEIGHBOURHOODS

ÖSTERMALM, GÄRDET & LADUGÅRDSGÄRDET

# >KUNGSHOLMEN

Upstaged by its most famous resident, the towering Stadshuset, little-known Kungsholmen is fast becoming Stockholm's quiet achiever. The island's blue-rinse set is making way for cool urban types escaping Östermalm's and Södermalm's ever-soaring rents – think yummy mummies, loft-living urbanites and tousle-haired artists in vintage cardies. Sidestreets harbour design-shop gems, ex-factories house ubercool bars, and red-brick blocks lend a Brooklyn vibe. It's a long way from 'Starvation Island', the nickname Kungsholmen endured during the Industrial Revolution, when putrid factories and lice-ridden locals made the place a no-go zone. These days, the island is better known for its swinging bistros, quirky boutiques and sublime waterside jogs along Norr Mälarstrand. Low on sights but high on lifestyle, this is the kind of place where hip young shopkeepers know each other, recommend each other and knock back a beer together. Chances are you'll end up toasting the old 'K' too.

## KUNGSHOLMEN

# SEE

## STADSHUSET

☎ 50 82 90 58; Hantverkargatan 1; adult/under 12yr/12-17yr/concession Skr70/free/40/60, Stockholm Card free; ⏱ 45min guided tours in English 10am, noon, 2pm May & Sep, hourly 10am-3pm Jun-Aug, 10am & noon daily, 2pm Sat & Sun Oct-Apr; Ⓜ T-Centralen

Built in the National Romantic style using eight million bricks and completed in 1923, Stockholm's iconic City Hall is home of the Nobel Banquet, held in the Italianate Blue Hall, which is in fact red. More accurately named is the Golden Hall, a glittering spectacle made with 10kg of gold and 68 million mosaic pieces. Tours of the building are fascinating, while a soulful chill on the waterside terrace (the sculptures are by Carl Eldh) is free. For breathtaking views over Gamla Stan, head to the top of the hulking **tower** (adult/child Skr30/free; ⏱ 10am-4pm May & Sep, 9am-5pm Jun-Aug). That the tower is exactly 1m taller than Copenhagen's slightly older City Hall tower is no coincidence – neighbourly rivalries are hard to quench.

## TULLMUSEET

☎ 653 05 03; www.tullverket.se/en/museum; Alströmergatan 39; admission free; ⏱ 11am-4pm Tue, Wed & Sun; Ⓜ Fridhemsplan

Despite the patchy availability of English-language information, the Customs Museum is worth a snoop for its rather revealing exhibition on the 'art' of smuggling, which includes a pair of spacious knickers used to smuggle alcohol in the 1920s. Crack-stuffed sneakers aside, there's also a reconstruction of a

Stadshuset, Stockholm's impressive City Hall

1920s customs warehouse and lab with eerily realistic mannequins.

 # SHOP

### 📷 59 VINTAGE STORE
*Vintage Fashion*

☎ 652 37 27; Hantverkargatan 59;
☙ noon-7pm Mon-Fri, 12-4pm Sat;
Ⓜ Rådhuset

This rack-packed nirvana of retro threads will have you playing dress-up for hours. Both girls and boys can expect high-quality gear from the 1950s to the 1970s, including glam mid-century ballgowns, platform boots, Brit-pop blazers, *Dr Zhivago* faux-fur hats and the odd sequined sombrero.

### 📷 DEFYRA *Design*

☎ 650 76 06; www.defyra.nu; Bergsgatan 18; ☙ noon-6pm Fri; Ⓜ Rådhuset

This quirky design quartet has exhibited everywhere, from Manhattan and Tokyo to hotel lobbies at home. The gallery-shop features a giant hanging plastic bib and a playful collection of silkscreen-printed children's sweaters, T-shirts, hand-printed postcards and wallpapers, sublime ceramic teacups and stools made from severed skis.

### 📷 FRANK FORM
*Design & Fashion*

☎ 54 55 05 00; www.frankform
.se in Swedish; Kungsholmsgatan 20;
☙ 11.30am-7pm Mon-Fri, 11am-5pm
Sat; Ⓜ Rådhuset

Fetching interior design, fashion and jewellery you're unlikely to find elsewhere in town, including pieces from the UK, Spain and the Czech Republic. Pick up slinky guys' sweaters from Basque label Loreak Mendian, a classic handbag from Irish designer Orla Kiely or one-off jewellery from Swedish designer Jezebel, commissioned specially for the store.

### 📷 GRANDPA
*Clothing & Accessories*

☎ 643 60 81; Fridhemsgatan 43;
☙ 11am-7pm Mon-Fri, to 6pm Sat,
noon-4pm Sun; Ⓜ Fridhemsplan

**Lydia Kellam**
*Editor, The Swede Beat e-magazine (www.theswedebeat.com)*

**What is the Swede Beat?** The Swede Beat is an online magazine/newsletter born out of my dream of connecting my two worlds: Sweden and the US. I found a huge interest for Swedish music, fashion and design after moving to New York. People knew a lot of about Swedish bands and brands, but they didn't know they actually were from Sweden. Being proud of my home country I wanted everyone to know, and I handed out Swedish mix tapes at my internship at CMJ Network. **What's Swedish music like today?** Eclectic and creative. The Swedish cultural scene in general is very open to international influences, which makes the content very accessible for international audiences. It makes the music innovative, mixing genres and styles. **Top 5 albums?** These are talents I believe you should keep an eye on right now and in the future:  Jenny Wilson, *Hardship;* Lykke Li, *Youth Novels;* Veronica Maggio, *Och vinnaren är…*; Jens Lekman, *Night Falls over Kortedala*; and First Aid Kit, *Drunken Trees.*

With a design inspired by the hotels of the French Riviera during the '70s, Grandpa's second Stockholm location is crammed with atmosphere, as well as artfully chosen vintage and faux-vintage clothing, cool and quirky accessories and whatnots, random hairdryers, suitcases and old radios, plus a cool little cafe serving good espresso.

### ☐ LA NINJA *Novelty*

☎ 785 06 09; www.laninja.se in Swedish; Polhemsgatan 21; ☽ 11am-7pm Mon-Fri, noon-4pm Sat & Sun; Ⓜ Rådhuset

Off-the-wall indie design from Sweden and beyond, including comic-print wallets, pop-art clogs, super-kitsch Anne Taintor tote bags and fairy-tale tank tops from Singapore's Lynda Lye. The retro-print bedsheets from Farg Form are a huge hit with nostalgic generation-X Swedes. The owner's mum can snip your hair next door.

### ☐ ROOM *Design*

☎ 692 50 00; www.room.se; Alströmergatan 20; ☽ 10am-6.30pm Mon-Fri, 10am-5pm Sat, 11am-5pm Sun; Ⓜ Fridhemsplan

This huge interior-design store is a hit with cashed-up urbanites who seem to spend entire weekends here matching up fabrics and weighing up the pros and cons of Nigella Lawson salad servers for the kitchen. Get in the vibe or simply opt for a Manolo Blahnik shoehorn and kick back in the buzzing cafe.

### ☐ SOUNDKILLA
*Records & Music*

☎ 654 14 00; www.soundkillarecords .com; St Eriksgatan 48; ☽ noon-6pm Mon-Fri, noon-4pm Sat; Ⓜ Fridhemsplan

This hole-in-the-wall record shop gets down to reggae, man, from old-school dancehall to ska, roots, dub and revival. Weekly imports from Jamaica, the UK and the US keep the DJs rolling in, and owner Ashman is your man for the lowdown on Stockholm's reggae party scene.

### ☐ VÄSTERMALMSGALLERIAN
*Shopping Centre*

☎ 737 20 00; www.vastermalms gallerian.se; St Eriksgatan 45; ☽ 10am-7pm Mon-Fri, 10am-5pm Sat, 11am-5pm Sun; Ⓜ Fridhemsplan

This busy mall is home to some noteworthy residents. Pick up Scandi-design at **DesignTorget** ( ☎ 33 11 53; www.designtorget.se), sexy Swedish briefs at **Björn Borg** ( ☎ 652 12 40; www.bjornborg.se), cult cosmetics at **Face Stockholm** ( ☎ 650 01 56; www .facestockholm.com) and democratically priced kids' and women's threads at **H&M** ( ☎ 54 57 22 90; www.hm.com).

NEIGHBOURHOODS

KUNGSHOLMEN

#  EAT

Kungsholmen is getting quite a reputation for its dining scene. Some of the city's current darlings line its shore and streets, from designer Thomas Sandell's Kungsholmen to the Le Marais cool of Bergamott. Best of all, most are off the tourist track, so you'll be chewing and clinking smugly.

### ALLMÄNNA GALLERIET 925
*Swedish-French* €€€
☎ 41 06 81 00; www.ag925.se; Kronobergsgatan 37; ⏰ 5pm-1am Tue-Sun; Ⓜ Fridhemsplan

AG925 has all the 'it kid' prerequisites – obscure urban location (ex–silver factory), post-industrial fit-out (concrete floors, white-tiled walls, Tom Dixon lights), hip bar (saggy Chesterfields, competent cocktails) and classic grub with a modern twist (baked wood pigeon with potato and apple hash). Add impeccable service, edgy art shows and a metropolitan vibe and expect a long-term addiction.

### BERGAMOTT
*French-Italian* €€€
☎ 650 30 34; Hantverkargatan 35; ⏰ 5.30pm-midnight Mon-Sat; Ⓜ Rådhuset

The three very cool French chefs in the kitchen don't simply whip up to-die-for French-Italian dishes,

they'll probably deliver them to your table, talk you through the produce and guide you through the wine list. It's never short of a convivial crowd, so it's best to book, especially when jazz musicians drop in for a soulful evening jam.

### IL CAFFÈ *Cafe* €
☎ 652 30 04; www.ilcaffe.se in Swedish; Bergsgatan 17; ⏰ 8am-6pm Mon-Fri, 10am-6pm Sat & Sun; Ⓜ Rådhuset

Low-strung lights, angst-ridden writers and edgy graphic murals by Stockholm graffiti artist Finsta (www.finstafari.com) load this local hangout with boho grit. Italian-leaning lunch options include authentic focaccias – try the pesto/mozzarella combo, made to an old-school Italian recipe. Finish off with a jumbo-sized caffè latte, then flip out that Moleskine and work on that plot.

### KUNGSHOLMEN
*International* €€€
☎ 50 52 44 50; www.kungsholmen.com; Norr Mälarstrand, Kajplats 464; ⏰ 5pm-midnight Mon-Wed, 5pm-2am Thu-Sat, 3-10pm Sun; Ⓜ Rådhuset

Owned by celebrity chef Melker Andersson (F12, p76; Grill, p71), this sexed-up food court features six open kitchens cooking up six specialties – soup, sushi, grill, bistro, bread or ice cream. Add a sleek long bar offering a huge range

## POLAR BARE

These days you'll find a glossy gym at No 58 St Eriksgatan. Between 1978 and 2004, however, this was the home of the legendary Polar Studios – Stockholm's version of Memphis' Sun Studios and London's Abbey Road. Established by ABBA's Benny Andersson, Bjorn Ulvaeus, and band manager Stig Anderson, the five-studio complex was where the pop quartet recorded their final three albums – *Voulez-Vous* (1979), *Super Trouper* (1980) and *The Visitors* (1981).

It was also where Led Zeppelin recorded their album *In Through the Out Door* (1978), alongside a league of other big-name acts including the Rolling Stones, the Beastie Boys, Genesis, Roxette and the Cardigans. While Stig Anderson sold the facility in 1984, it was soaring rents that forced the studio to 'ad lib to fade' in 2004.

of elaborate cocktails as well as simpler fare like pints of Brooklyn Lager, weekend DJs and a languid lakeside setting, and you'll understand why it's best to book.

### 🍴 LUX DESSERT OCH CHOKLAD *Chocolate & Pastries* €

☎ 656 20 20; www.luxdessertochchoklad.com; Patentgatan 7; ⏱ 9am-7pm Tue-Fri, 9am-4pm Sat & Sun; 🚌 49
Little brother to Lux Stockholm, this is the haute patisserie of celebrated confectioner Ted Johansson, who devised the dessert menu for the 2005 Nobel Banquet. Throw your scales to the wind.

### 🍴 LUX STOCKHOLM
*New Swedish* €€€

☎ 619 01 90; www.luxstockholm.com; Primusgatan 116; ⏱ lunch 11.30am-2pm Tue-Fri, dinner 5-11pm Tue-Sat; 🚌 49
Lux by name, luxe by nature, this Michelin-star hotspot is run by Bocuse d'Or silver medal winner Hen-

rik Norström. Expect obscenely original creations like spiced lobster with almond milk and duck with pistachio and ginger, all served in what was once the Electrolux factory canteen. Needless to say, book ahead (by the window in winter, on the terrace in summer).

### 🍴 ROPPONGI *Japanese* €€€

☎ 650 17 72; www.roppongi.se in Swedish; Hantverkargatan 76; ⏱ 11am-10pm Mon-Fri, 1-10pm Sat, 1-9pm Sun; Ⓜ Fridhemsplan
It might be a long way to Tokyo, but you'd never know it at this sushi star. From the succulent swordfish okonomi to the Kubota sake, it's all top-notch and craved by faithful locals, so book ahead for dinner.

### 🍴 TABBOULI *Lebanese* €€€

☎ 650 25 00; www.tabbouli.lunchinfo.com in Swedish; Norra Agnegatan 39; ⏱ 5-11pm Mon-Thu, 5pm-midnight Fri & Sat; Ⓜ Rådhuset

Waterside terrace, Stadshuset (p128)

This Middle Eastern maverick ditches stock-standard neon lights and greasy kebabs for decadent wine-red drapes, hanging silks and lavish Lebanese creations like spicy marinated peppers and walnuts and perfectly fried chickpea cakes. If you're in company, opt for the brilliant banquets for that full-on harem feeling.

### 🍴 THELINS KONDITORI
Cafe €
☎ 651 19 00; St Eriksgatan 43; 🕑 7.30am-7pm Mon-Fri, 9am-5pm Sat, 10am-5pm Sun; Ⓜ Fridhemsplan
Traditional Thelins sits precariously on the line between charm

and tack – think '70s coffee shop meets red velvet seating and faux-Parisian streetlamps. Less contentious are the gems behind the gleaming counter, from flaky berry-filled pastries to sinfully satisfying semla buns. Take a ticket, join the queue and succumb to your sugar-dusted fantasies.

### 🍴 VURMA
Cafe €
☎ 650 93 50; www.vurma.se in Swedish; Polhemsgatan 15; 🕑 10am-6pm; Ⓜ Rådhuset
Squeeze in among the happy punters, fluff up the cushions and eavesdrop over a vegan latte and heavenly angel sandwich (cream cheese, avocado, turkey and Dijon mustard). The Vasastaden branch of **Vurma** ( ☎ 30 62 30; Gästrikegatan 2; 🕑 10am-6pm Mon-Fri, 11am-6pm Sat & Sun) draws a younger clientele and, as one waitress puts it, 'more flirt vibrations'.

# Ⓨ DRINK
### Ⓨ GÖKEN Gay & Lesbian
☎ 654 49 28; www.goken.nu in Swedish; Pontonjärgatan 28; 🕑 lunch 11am-2pm Mon-Fri, brunch noon-4pm Sun, dinner 5-10pm daily; Ⓜ Fridhemsplan
From the handbag house to the handbag lamp on the bar, friendly laid-back Göken (Cuckoo) is camper than a jamboree. The bleach-blond barman looks like

## THE VODKA KING

In 1897 industrialist Lars Olsson Smith developed a new filtering method (rectification), which rid strong liquor of the terrible taste of ethanol. The result was a cleaner vodka Smith christened 'Absolut Rent Brännvin' (absolute pure vodka) and the birth of a Swedish icon, Absolut Vodka. Originally planning to call his vodka either 'Swedish Blonde Vodka', 'Swedish Black Vodka' or 'Damn Swede', Smith was determined to break the city's monopoly on selling the stuff, refusing to obtain a permit to sell his new liquor in Stockholm and instead opening his own shop next to his distillery on Reimersholme, just outside the city limits. Adding insult to injury, he offered Stockholmers a free shuttle-boat ride to his island shop. Smith's brilliant marketing plan won him the dubious title 'The King of Vodka'.

he's walked straight out of *La Cage aux Folles* and the friendly gay/straight crowd perfectly complements the ab fab cocktail list. Take the barman's advice and try a Boeing.

### Y LEMON BAR *Bar*
☎ 650 17 78; Scheelegatan 8;
Ⓜ Rådhuset
A favourite among locals for its laid-back vibe, the Lemon Bar epitomises the kind of comfy neighbourhood joint you can drop into on the spur of the moment and count on finding a friendly crowd and good music, mostly Swedish pop hits that may or may not result in dancing.

### Y M/S GERDA BAR
*Floating Bar*
☎ 650 80 31; MS Gerda, Norr Mälarstrand, Kajplatser 466; ⏰ 11am-1am Mon-Fri, noon-1am Sat & Sun summer; Ⓜ Rådhuset

While the nosh at neighbouring Kungsholmen (p132) wins hands down, this sassy floating bar is a fine place to sip daiquiris and catch a summer breeze. The playground of professional types (some of whom arrive by private boat), it's also a good place to snag yourself a cashed-up Swedish plaything.

### Y MÄLARPAVILJONGEN
*Bistro & Bar*
☎ 650 87 01; www.malarpaviljongen .se in Swedish; Norr Mälarstrand 63; ⏰ 11am-midnight Apr-early Oct; Ⓜ Fridhemsplan
When the sun comes out to play, few places beat this alfresco lakeside resto-bar for some Nordic *dolce vita*. Mixed during the day and mostly gay at night, it features bistro-style grub, a cosy glassed-in gazebo over the water and a darn good raspberry fudge cocktail. Call ahead for opening times, which are affected by the weather.

### ☑ TERRENOS VINOTEK
*Wine Bar*

☎ 653 19 88; www.terrenosvinotek.se
in Swedish; Scheelegatan 12; ⏰ 5-11pm
Wed-Thu, 5pm-midnight Fri & Sat;
Ⓜ Rådhuset

This slick Italian-style wine bar
sells its wares by the centilitre,
which is just as well considering
the fine wines on offer. Sip your
way from South Africa to Spain,
and enjoy the trip with rustic
Italian cheeses or a serving of
carpaccio.

## ⭐ PLAY

⭐ FRIA TEATREN *Theatre*

☎ 99 22 60; www.friateatern.se in
Swedish; Bergsgatan 11; tickets Skr150-
200; Ⓜ Rådhuset

Although its main base is in the
suburbs, this independent theatre
company also treads the boards
here at Lilla Scenen, its affiliated
stage. Born in the heady days of
1968, modest Fria has built up a
mighty reputation for top-notch
work with an often biting political
edge.

### ⭐ RÅLAMBSHOVSPARKEN
*Park*

In the warmer months, Rålambs-
hovsparken is one of the city's
favourite playgrounds, packed
with picnicking Swedes fresh from
a dip in the lake. Take a swim,
hire a canoe or just get physical
at the free alfresco aerobics sessions, nightly at 6pm through the
summer.

# >STOCKHOLM ARCHIPELAGO

While the number of islands is debatable (anything between 14,000 and 100,000, with the general consensus being 24,000), the beauty of the archipelago (p20) is indisputable. Its buffed isles, fields of wild flowers and deep blue waters have sparked the muse for the likes of August Strindberg, Carl Larsson and Anders Zorn. Regular ferry services from Stockholm mean it can do the same for you. Of the various ferry companies, Waxholmsbolaget runs the most services. Your best source of information on the islands is the region's custodial body, the Archipelago Foundation (www.skargardsstiftelsen.se), which produces several useful guides on the area.

Cruise the clear waters to the archipelago islands

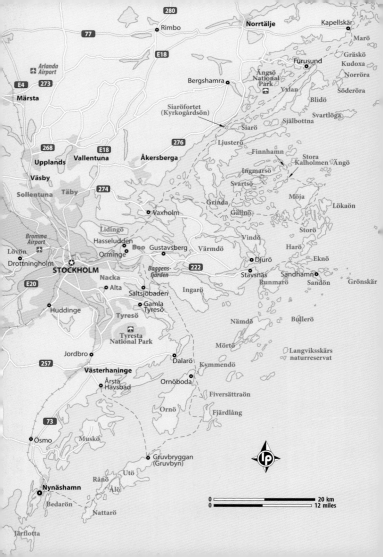

# VAXHOLM

Despite the ice cream–licking summer hordes, Vaxholm redeems itself with its easy accessibility, storybook summerhouses and historic Norrhamn district, a few minutes' walk north of the town hall. It's also the gateway to the archipelago's central and northern reaches.

Its most famous icon is the hulking fortress **Vaxholm Kastell** ( ☎ 54 17 21 57; www.vaxholmsfastning.se; adult/under 18yr Skr50/free; ✸ noon-4pm daily Jun, 11am-5pm daily Jul & Aug, 11am-5pm Sat & Sun early Sep), set on an unnamed islet just east of the town. Originally ordered by Gustav Vasa in 1544, it came under attack by the Danes in 1612 and the Russian navy in 1719; most of the current structure dates from 1863. Nowadays it's home to the National Museum of Coastal Defence.

Back in the town, mosey down Hamngatan, lined with galleries, boutiques and (in summer) happy sunburnt Swedes.

For a fix of olde-worlde appeal, head to open-air museum **Hembygdsgård** ( ☎ 54 13 17 20; Trädgårdsgatan 19; admission free; ✸ noon-4pm Sat & Sun Jun-Aug), which puts on the charm with the finest old houses in Vaxholm, including the *fiskarebostad*, an excellent example of a late-19th-century fisherman's house.

For food, try **Melanders Fisk** ( ☎ 54 13 34 66; Hamngatan 2), **Waxholms Hotel** ( ☎ 54 13 01 50; Hamngatan 2), **Hamnkrogen** ( ☎ 54 13 20 39; Södermhamnen 10) and **Café Galleri Linderholm** ( ☎ 54 13 21 65; www.linderholm.se).

## INFORMATION
**Location** 35km northeast of Stockholm
**Getting there** Ⓜ Tekniska Högskolan, then bus 670. Waxholmsbolaget ferries (Map pp52–3, G6; ☎ 679 58 30; www.waxholmsbolaget.se; one way Skr75; one hour) sail frequently between Vaxholm and Strömkajen in Stockholm, with around 20 to 30 services daily in the high season. See the website for timetables.
**Contact** www.vaxholm.se, Archipelago Foundation ( ☎ 440 56 00; www.skargardsstiftelsen.se)
**When to go** May to September

### GUNNAR HJERTSTRAND
*Archipelago Foundation Ranger*

**Favourite spot in the archipelago** The outer islands. They're stark, wind-swept and hauntingly beautiful. Uninhabited Grönskär is home to the 'Queen of the Baltic', a beautiful stone lighthouse built in 1770. To reach the island, book a water taxi from Sandön (Sandhamns Båttaxi; ☎ 57 15 35 55). The lighthouse itself is usually open on Sundays in July, weather permitting. **Look out for** Colonies of grey seals in the early summer, especially in the outer archipelago. Stricter environmental controls over the past few decades have seen their numbers increase from 3000 to 20,000 in the region. **Don't miss** The archipelago in winter. The crowds have gone, the islands are peaceful and the frozen waters make for wonderful skating and skiing. **Top tip** Although ferries to the archipelago leave from central Stockholm, it's quicker to take a bus to ports like Vaxholm and Stavsnäs and catch the ferries out from there.

# SANDÖN

Sandön is the archipelago's summertime party hotspot. Stockholm status slaves save all year just to sail in on a 12-footer for a midsummer weekend of schmoozing and boozing. Serious sailors also flock here for regattas like the Gotland Rund each July.

A manageable 2.5km wide, the island's hub is the northern settlement of Sandhamn. Here, narrow alleys, rust-red cottages and the Royal Swedish Yacht Club's Hamptons-style clubhouse keep the cameras clicking. In the clubhouse you'll find **Seglarrestaurangen** ( ☎ 57 45 04 21; www.sandhamn.com; ☺ year-round), one of the archipelago's best restaurants. Two other nearby gems are trendy **Dykarbaren** ( ☎ 57 15 35 54; www.dykarbaren.se; Sandhamn Eknö 1; ☺ May-Sep) and **Sandhamns Värdshus** ( ☎ 57 15 30 51; www.sandhamns-vardshus.se; ☺ Apr–mid-Dec); the latter has been serving up wild game and seafood since 1672.

Despite the island's penchant for urbane comforts (camping is prohibited), Sandön flaunts some fabulous Med-style beaches, the best of the lot near the southern tip at Trovill, a 20-minute walk through cool pine forests. Of course, if you prefer to swim, steam and sip simultaneously, opt for the spa retreat at **Seglarhotellet** ( ☎ 57 45 04 00; www.sandhamn.com; pool pass Skr100; ☺ pool daily year-round, spa centre Wed-Sun Jul–mid-Aug, Fri-Sun mid-Aug–Jun), complete with pool-side bar.

## INFORMATION

**Location** 48km east of Stockholm
**Getting there** In the high season, Waxholmsbolaget ferries ( ☎ 679 58 30; www.waxholmsbolaget.se; one way Skr130, three hours, once daily) sail from Strömkajen to Sandhamn. A better option is to take 🚌 433 or 🚌 434 from Slussen to Stavsnäs (50 minutes) and catch a ferry from there (one way Skr75, one hour, six to nine times daily in the high season). Check the website for departure times. Strömma Kanalbolaget ( ☎ 58 71 40 00; www.stromma.se) runs tours from Nybroplan to Sandhamn daily between early June and late August (one way/return Skr210/280), departing at 9.30am and returning at 5.30pm, with two hours on Sandhamn (including a one-hour guided walk).
**Contact** www.skargardsstiftelsen.se
**When to go** Year-round

# FINNHAMN

Despite its popularity, languid Finnhamn never loses its eco-cool. It's made up of compact, interconnecting islands protected by the Archipelago Foundation, and its youth hostel, restaurant and summertime grocery store are happily outnumbered by shady woods, sheltered coves, lush meadows, smooth rocky cliffs and visiting eagle owls.

The hostel, housed in a yellow wooden villa designed by Ernst Stenhammar in 1912, rents out rowing boats and boats with outboards for lazy island hopping, while its little seaside sauna lets you sweat it out with Nordic aqua views.

The islands' name (literally, Finnish Harbour) pays tribute to the Finnish boats that regularly stopped here on their way to and from Stockholm.

As on many islands protected by the Archipelago Foundation, you can camp in the woods for free for two days without the need to advise the islands' landlord.

For food, try **Finnhamn Café Krog** (☎ 54 24 64 04; Stora Jolpan; ⏲ Easter-Oct).

### THE RIGHT OF PUBLIC ACCESS

The Swedish custom of *allemansrätten* ('Everyman's Right') allows you to walk, ski, boat or swim anywhere outside private property as long you stay at least 70m from houses and keep out of gardens, fenced areas and cultivated land. You can also pick nonprotected berries and mushrooms and camp in the wild for that wholesome Scandi feeling. Check www.allemansratten.se for details.

## INFORMATION

**Location** 45km northeast of Stockholm
**Getting there** Waxholmsbolaget ferries (☎ 679 58 30; www.waxholmsbolaget.se; Skr130; 2½ hours) sail from Strömkajen (Stockholm) to Finnhamn, via Vaxholm, up to seven times daily in the high season, fewer in the low season. Scan the website for times.
**Contact** www.finnhamn.se
**When to go** Year-round

# GRINDA

With its perfect swimming spots, luscious forests and curiously cute Swedish sheep, little Grinda is a seasoned people-pleaser. Located little more than an hour away by boat from Stockholm, it also makes for an easy daytrip from town.

In 1906, the island was bought by Henrik Santesson, the first director of the Nobel Foundation. Santesson commissioned architect Ernst Stenhammar to design him a summer holiday pad. One can only imagine Santesson's holiday mood was dampened when his wife, Alfhild, drowned herself in the sea below.

Thankfully, happy days are back and the elegant art nouveau number now houses the award-scooping restaurant-hotel **Grinda Wärdshus** ( ☎ 54 24 94 91; www.grindawardshus.se; ⏰ year-round, bookings essential Oct-Apr). The fresh seasonal menus here have won many fans, from *Gourmet Magazine* to famous customer Bjorn Ulvaeus. The ABBA icon has two homes on the neighbouring island of Viggsö, where he and band member Benny Andersson penned many an ABBA hit.

If you forget to book ahead (or if you're kronor-economising), bag a table at **Framfickan** (Front Pocket; ☎ 54 24 94 91; ⏰ late May-early Sep). Located by the guest harbour, just down the slope from its grander neighbour, this bistro-style hangout is a summertime hit for simple, good, cheaper grub right by the Baltic Sea.

If you're longing for a dip, ditch the cliff-clad eastern shores for sandy west side Källviken. Equally good is the splash-friendly northern shore. Sun or snow, hit the rambling walking tracks for bucolic staples, including soft pines, old red timber barns…and did we mention those cute Swedish sheep?

## INFORMATION

**Location** 25km northeast of Stockholm
**Getting there** Waxholmsbolaget ferries ( ☎ 679 58 30; www.waxholmsbolaget.se; Skr90, 1½ hours) runs up to 10 daily ferries to Grinda from Strömkajen (Stockholm) in the high season, with less frequent services in the low season. See the website for timetables.
**Contact** www.grindawardshus.se
**When to go** Year-round

# >SNAPSHOTS

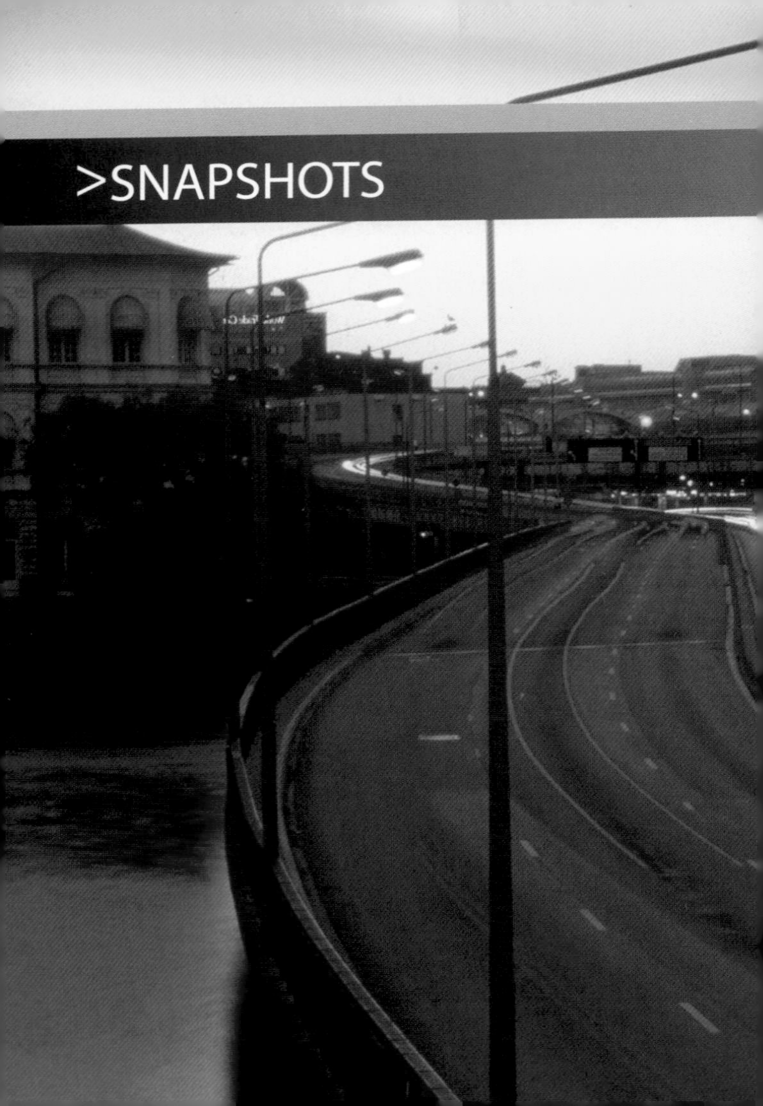

Like any intriguing personality, Stockholm is a multifaceted being — *schlager*-happy, symphony-savvy, indie smart and slavishly chic. One minute it's cool and blonde, the next it's sexy, streetsmart and jamming. Snapshots offer sharp, tasty glimpses of all its best angles, from designer slumber and noshing to born-again buildings and multi-ethnic beats.

Stockholm on the move

# ACCOMMODATION

Once notorious for drab business hotels, Stockholm finally raised the slumber stakes several years ago. Hot designer hotels like rock-star refuge **Berns** (www.berns.se), ubersleek **Clarion** (www.clarionstockholm.com) and film-themed **Rival** (www.rival.se) now grace the pages of design mag *Wallpaper* so that crashing has become a cutting-edge pleasure.

Indeed, many of these pads have become virtual odes to Swedish designers; **Birger Jarl** (www.birgerjarl.se) showcases different homegrown talent in its suites, while the minimalist **Nordic Light Hotel** (www.nordiclighthotel.se) – insist on a corner room on the 10th floor – is a veritable gallery of light installations. More low-key but equally designer-conscious is the **Art Hotel** (arthotel@telia.com), inspired by London's Chelsea Arts Club and Amsterdam's De Filosoof, and a predictable hit with the creative types.

For traditional glamour, the **Grand Hôtel** (www.grandhotel.se) trumps the competition. Crammed with royal Gustavian furnishings and celebrity anecdotes (see boxed text, p92), it's the Stockholm equivalent of New York's Waldorf Astoria.

Of course, those on a humbler budget needn't fret. Fleapits are hard to find in this city and even the humblest hostel is generally comfy, clean and capably staffed. Several hostels boast fetching locations, from **Vandrarhem Af Chapman's** (www.stfchapman.com) renovated 19th-century sailing ship to **Långholmen Hotell & Vandrarhem's** (www.langholmen.com) converted island prison.

A room at a hostel will cost between Skr185 and Skr575 per person, depending on whether you choose a dorm bed or a private room. A

Need a place to stay? Find and book it at lonelyplanet.com. More than 135 properties are featured for Stockholm – each personally visited, thoroughly reviewed and happily recommended by a Lonely Planet author. From hostels to high-end hotels, we've hunted out the places that will bring you unique and special experiences. Read independent reviews by authors and other travellers, and get practical information including amenities, maps and photos. Then reserve your room simply and securely via Hotels & Hostels – our online booking service. It's all at lonelyplanet.com/hotels.

Hostelling International (HI) card will give you discounts on Svenska Turistföreningen (STF) hostel rates; you can buy a card at any of the youth hostels for Skr295.

Prices at major hotels are typically Skr1500 to Skr2000 per night for a double room, although the listed price is rarely the lowest available. Nearly all hotel room prices drop by up to 50% on weekends and during July, so always ask about special deals and discounts when booking a room.

Another plus is the city's compact size. Coupled with efficient public transport, it means that where you choose to stay isn't as crucial as it would be in London or LA. That said, Södermalm is best for New Swedish fashion and indie-cool bars, Östermalm is the city's A-list clubbing hub, Gamla Stan heaves with historic charm and central Norrmalm is handy for airport trains and buses. For a decadent minivacation outside the city, book yourself a *ryokan* suite at Japanese spa retreat Hasseludden Konferens & Yasuragi (see boxed text, p120).

Those planning a longer Stockholm sojourn (or simply a spot of cooking) will find quality longer-term rentals at www.checkin.se. Equally useful is www.destination-stockholm.com, a discount hotel-and-sightseeing package site with deals on some of the city's top hotels in the off season. For last-minute accommodation bookings, contact the **Stockholm Visitors Board** (Map pp52-3, G5; ☎ 50 82 85 08; www.stockholmtown.com; Hamngatan 27; 🕑 9am-7pm Mon-Fri, 9am-5pm Sat, 10am-4pm Sun; Ⓜ T-Centralen).

---

### BEST FOR...

> **Old-school opulence** Grand Hôtel (www.grandhotel.se)
> **Party people** Berns Hotel (www.berns.com)
> **Summer house chilling** J Sealodge Gåshaga (www.hotelj.com)
> **Faded glamour** Hotel Esplanade (www.hotelesplanade.se)
> **Luxe views at a low price** Vandrarhem Af Chapman (www.stfchapman.com)

### TOP FIVE DESIGN HOTELS

> Nordic Light Hotel (www.nordiclighthotel.se)
> Clarion Hotel (www.clarionstockholm.com)
> Rival Hotel (www.rival.se)
> Birger Jarl (www.birgerjarl.se)
> Hotel Hellsten (www.hellsten.se)

# SHOPPING

From too-cool crockery to street-smart threads, Stockholm's style obsession makes for serious shopping satisfaction. Cool local buys include home-grown fashion (p150), designer homewares (p157), handmade glassware and edible treats like cloudberry jam, *lingonsylt* (lingonberry jam), bottles of Blossa *glögg* at Christmas and pickled herring in *brännvin* (aquavit) sauce – assuming you can get it past customs at the other end. For the best Nordic grub, head to Östermalms Saluhall (p15) and Hötorgshallen (p68) – Stockholm's lip-smacking gastro-markets.

For handicrafts without the chintz, don't miss Konsthantverkarna (p97), one of several stylish co-op craft shops. Blås & Knåda (p93) is another good bet for handmade Swedish design, especially glassware and ceramics; the gallery is on Hornsgatan, a street well known for its artisan studios and a great spot for picking up local designer jewellery and contemporary Swedish art. Also good are richly coloured Sami handicrafts from Lappland, which should sport a coloured Duodji label to confirm their authenticity.

Contrasting neighbourhoods offer different shopping vibes. Vintage Gamla Stan is the king of kitsch, its main thoroughfare Västerlånggatan swamped with shops selling Swedish flags and mini Vikings. Ditch it for savvier Österlånggatan (Map p37, E4) and the atmospheric side streets, where you'll find art galleries, craft studios and adorable one-off shops.

Downtown Norrmalm houses the main shopping malls and department stores, including landmark NK (pictured right; p62), as well as crowded pedestrian strip Drottninggatan (Map pp52–3, E5) and the flagship stores for leading Stockholm labels Acne (p59) and WESC (p63). In Vasastaden you'll find progressive jewellery at Platina (p63) and jaw-dropping junk shop Nostalgipalatset (p63). Further south is Record Hunter (p63), one of the city's best spots for CDs and well-priced vinyl.

Tourist-free Kungsholmen harbours some of the city's design heavyweights, like ROOM (p131) and Frank Form (p129), while ever-hip Södermalm has the city's best vintage clothing stores, secondhand record shops and well-designed streetwear from Stockholm's emerging fashion stars.

Across town, Östermalm is the spot for high-end retail therapy, from catwalk couture on Birger Jarlsgatan (Map pp52–3, G5) to cult design on Sibyllegatan (Map pp110-11, C4). For a totally different shopping adventure, forage around at a neighbourhood market, where you can mingle with locals rifling through vintage fashion, jewellery and knicknacks. Further south in the suburbs, Skärholmen flea market (see boxed text, p98) is a cool spot for ethnic exotica and quirky secondhand finds.

In December, don't miss the city's atmospheric Christmas markets (*julmarknand*) – there are excellent ones in Gamla Stan's Stortorget (Map p37, D3) and Skansen (p80) on Djurgården.

Across Stockholm, stores are generally open 10am to 6pm or 7pm Monday to Friday, 10am to 4pm Saturday and noon to 4pm Sunday. Some hyper-fashionable boutiques open at 11am or noon on weekdays, while supermarkets often open and close later. On the last Thursday of every month, several shops in Södermalm's SoFo district open until 9pm. If it's wine or spirits you're after, visit a Systembolaget store (www.systembolaget.se), open normal store hours from Monday to Friday, and until 3pm Saturday.

Non-EU residents are entitled to a duty-free refund of up to 17.5% on single purchases of more than Skr200 bought from tax-free shopping outlets. (Look for a 'Tax Free' sticker on doors or by the register, ask the salesperson, or pick up a Tax Free Shopping Guide to Sweden at the tourist office.)

An even better way to save money is to hit the stores after Christmas when nearly all the shops in town have massive end-of-year sales from 27 to 29 December. Some sales stretch into early January, meaning 75% off a pair of Cesare Paciotti sneakers needn't be a fashionista fantasy.

### TOP FIVE SHOPPING STREETS
> Drottninggatan (Map pp52–3, E5)
> Biblioteksgatan (Map pp110–11, B5)
> Hamngatan (Map pp52–3, G5)
> Götgatan (Map pp88–9, F3)
> Österlånggatan (Map p37, E3)

### TOP FIVE SWEDISH MUST-BUYS
> Snaps
> Acne Jeans
> Peter Björn & John CD
> Pippi Longstocking picture book
> Dalarna wooden horse

# FASHION

Swedish fashion is on a roll. Since the late 1990s, the local scene has become one of the world's coolest. Madonna dons Patrik Söderstam trousers and new-season Acne jeans (p59) sell like hotcakes at LA's mega-hip Fred Segal. Sweden now exports more fashion than pop and the newest academic discipline at Stockholm University is fashion studies.

As the country's style hub, Stockholm boasts most of the flagship stores and emerging talent. Fashion stalwarts include Anna Holtblad (p115), J Lindeberg (p116) and the sombre chic of Filippa K (p115). Street-wise label WESC (p63) is hot in Hollywood, while minimalist Whyred (p64) is a hit with the local style council.

For Scandi-cool sans the hefty price tag, raid the racks at H&M (p61), where previous guest designers have included Stella McCartney, Viktor & Rolf and Madonna. In 2007 the chain paid tribute to Australian style icon Kylie Minogue with its summer beachwear collection, 'H&M loves Kylie'. In 2008 fashion fans fell in love with the revamped PUB department store (Map pp52–3) on Hötorget, which is set to become a centre for niche local and international labels. Across the water in Södermalm, mini-mall Brunogallerian (p93) is already seducing the trendsetters, while close by the SoFo district (see boxed text, p94) is the city's epicentre for emerging and cutting-edge labels. Don't miss cult boutiques like Grandpa (p95, p129) and fashion cognoscenti darling Tjallamalla (p99), which stock new generation names like Patrik Söderstam, Pudel, Hope, So Last Season, Fifth Avenue Shoe Repair and House of Dagmar. Established by Anna Angseryd, Patouf (www.patouf.se) bagged the 2009 Rookie of the Year award at **Rookies & Players** (www.rookies.nu), a twice-yearly fashion event kick-started by the Swedish Fashion Council to spotlight new talent. The February edition of Rookies & Players takes place during **Stockholm Fashion Week** (www.style.stofair.se), Scandinavia's biggest fashion fair. It's an invite-only affair, although edgier indie fashion shows are sometimes held on Södermalm sidewalks and in SoFo shops during the monthly SoFo Nights. To tap into the local scene, check out www.stockholmfashion days.com, www.designsverige.blogspot.com, www.swedesres.typepad .com/blog/fashion/index.html and http://stockholmstreetstyle.feber.se (in Swedish).

## TOP FIVE FOR NEW SWEDISH FASHION
> Tjallamalla (p99)
> Acne (p59, p93)
> Grandpa (p95, p129)
> Gina Tricot (p95)
> Jus (p61)

## TOP FIVE STOCKHOLM LABELS
> Acne Jeans (www.acnejeans.com)
> Fifth Avenue Shoe Repair (www .shoerepair.se)
> Patrik Söderstam (www.patriksoder stam.com)
> Whyred (www.whyred.se)
> WESC (www.wesc.com)

## TOP FIVE SHOPS FOR VINTAGE THREADS
> Lisa Larssons (p97)
> Judits Second Hand (p97)
> Sivletto (p98)
> 59 Vintage Store (p129)
> Beyond Retro (p59)

**Opposite** Grandpa (p95, p129)

# DRINKING

When a city boasts a museum dedicated to grog – the Vin & Sprithis-toriska Museet (p58) in Stockholm's case – it comes as no surprise that its bar scene is sound and swinging. That said, most of the swinging in Stockholm happens on Thursday, Friday and Saturday nights, when locals head out en masse for a night on the tiles.

The bold and the beautiful strut straight to Östermalm and its Stureplan district, where design-savvy resto-bars like Riche (p122), Nox (p121), Viola (p122) and kicking Obaren (p121) set the scene for uberposh and maxi-priced sipping. Style up and head in by 10pm – after then, long queues and notoriously picky door bitches can quickly spoil your evening. Nearby, Norrmalm is home to blingy Berns Salonger (p72) and its hot underground bar/club 2.35:1, a current favourite with creative media types who like their Manhattans with a side serve of art projections. A merry swagger away is glitzy Café Opera (p71) and slinky summer hangout Fredsgatan 12 (p67).

For alternative cool sans attitude, head down south to Södermalm, Stockholm's capital of alcohol consumption. Bars here range from culture-vulture hangout Södra Teatern (p107) to lofty cocktail lounge Eriks Gondolen (p103) and left-wing beer hall Kvarnen (p104).

In the past few years, hotel bars have become the new cool. Once the domain of dreary decor and tragi-tourists, a new generation of styled-up spots like the Scandic Anglais (p122) and Rival (p105) have become choice hangouts for post-work wining.

Whether you opt for minimalist chic or indie intensity, the best thing about drinking in Stockholm is the way you order your beer. Rather than asking for a particular brand, since the mass-market Swedish beers are vir-tually indistinguishable from one another by flavour, you order by grade;

the usual order is a *storstark* – which translates to a 'big strong' and has an alcohol content of anything over 4.5%. (The meek can always opt for a *mellanöl*, or medium beer, with an alcohol content between 3.5% and 4.5%.) The weakest varieties, *folköl* (literally, 'people's beer') and *lättöl* (light beer) have an alcohol content of 2.25% to 3.5% and less than 2.5% respectively. Only the latter two can be purchased at supermarkets. The government's strict regulation of alcohol means the stronger varieties are available only in bars and the state-owned alcohol shops (see boxed text, p42).

The worst thing about drinking in Stockholm bars is the expense. Buying a round, even for good friends, is not a matter to be undertaken lightly. A *storstark* – typically an imperial pint of one of the cheap and uninspiring local mega-brew lagers, such as Spendrups, Pripps or Falcon – costs anywhere from Skr35 to Skr55, and imported beer or mixed drinks can be twice that amount. When browsing drink menus, be mindful that some of the prices listed may be per centilitre and not by the glass, making for a sobering bill for the unaware. To save money, locals often hold pre-drinking parties *(förfest)* at home, where the aim is to get tipsy before hitting the bars.

How long the party crowds can stay out varies from bar to bar, though most venues keep the punters partying to either 1am or 3am on Friday and Saturday nights. A number of spots around Stureplan keep pumping till 5am, though this is the exception rather than the rule.

One rule that was introduced in 2005 was a ban on smoking in Swedish bars and restaurants, which means you can now head home smelling like roses…or beer, at least.

---

**BEST FOR…**
> **Well-mixed drinks** Veranden @ Café Opera (p71)
> **Stylish sipping** Nox (p121)
> **Gritty urban chic** Allmänna Galleriet 925 (p132)
> **Picking up a local** Storstad (p72)
> **Unpretentious hanging-out** Nada (p104)
> **Old-school beer sessions** Kvarnen (p104)

> **In-crowd mingling** Riche (p122)
> **Bird's-eye views** Eriks Gondolen (p103)

**TOP FIVE SPOTS FOR ALFRESCO DRINKING**
> Mosebacke Etablissement (p106)
> Chokladkoppen & Kaffekoppen (p47)
> Fredsgatan 12 (p67)
> Mälarpaviljongen (p135)
> Sturehof (p119)

---

**Opposite** Brasserie Godot (p121)

# FOOD

In two decades, Stockholm has transformed itself from dining dowager to a confident gourmand. The capital boasts six Michelin-starred restaurants and its designer dining dens have become major city selling points.

Two current 'it' spots are elegant Esperanto (p65) and perennial favourite Leijontornet (p47), where tables are best booked weeks in advance. Along with the likes of Henrik Norström's Lux (p133) and Melker Andersson's Fredsgatan 12 (p67), they brilliantly personify new Swedish cuisine, a confident combo of seasonal produce and bold twists on classic cuisines, both local and global.

Ethnic flavours are also on the rise. While not yet up there with London or Melbourne for sheer variety and authenticity, the city harbours some worldly wonders, including Japanese joint Roppongi (p133), Chinese standby Ho's (p100) and Sichuan-Taiwanese Lao Wai (p68). The latter sits on Luntmakargatan, home to several top-notch Asian eateries.

As for old-school Swedish classics (husmanskost), fresh chefs have trimmed the fat, added the odd contemporary touch and won the old meatballs and gravadlax (cured salmon) a new legion of fans at spots like vintage Pelikan (p102).

Best of all, most nosh spots serve discounted lunch specials (dagens rätt) at a fixed price between 11.30am and 2pm Monday to Friday, which can mean A-list grub at digestible prices.

### BEST NEW-SWEDISH SENSATIONS
> Esperanto (p65)
> Lux (p133)
> Fredsgatan 12 (p67)

### BEST ETHNIC
> Abyssinia (p64)
> East (p118)
> Lao Wai (p68)
> Mooncake (p69)

### BEST RESTO-BAR COMBOS
> Allmänna Galleriet 925 (p132)
> Kungsholmen (p132)
> Landet (see boxed text, p84)
> Republik (p70)
> Sturehof (p119)

### BEST SWEET TREATS
> Chokladfabriken (p94)
> Lux Dessert och Choklad (p133)
> Thelins Konditori (p134)

# GALLERIES

Stockholm's love of all things fresh and new extends to the realm of art. While provocative stalwarts Färgfabriken (see boxed text, p101), Magasin 3 (p112) and Tensta Konsthall (see boxed text, p129) keep pushing the boundaries, contemporary galleries continue to sprout across the city, with Vasastaden proving a particularly fertile ground.

One of the biggest new players is Bonniers Konsthall (pictured below; p54), owned by media giant the Bonniers Group. Natalia Goldin Gallery (p55) is also a hit with a new generation of art buffs and neighbour to Brändström & Stene (p54), famed for showcasing the likes of Tracey Emin long before she hit the lifestyle mags.

Other gallery hotspots include Skeppargatan (Map pp110–11, C5) in Östermalm, the eastern end of Hornsgatan in Södermalm (Map pp88–9, E2), Österlanggatan (Map p37, E4) in Gamla Stan, and Skeppsholmen, home to Fotografins Hus (p78) and 20th-century heavyweight Moderna Museet (p12).

If you're in town in February, check out Stockholm's sharp art show, Market (p22). For Swedish (and international) art of a more classical persuasion, drop in at the venerable National Museum (p56) and waterside gems Prins Eugens Waldemarsudde (p80), Thielska Galleriet (p81) and Millesgården (p19).

To find out who's hanging in town, pick up a free copy of *Konstguiden* or the Svenska Dagbladet exhibition calendar at galleries, or click onto www.galleriforbundet.com or www.konsten.net (in Swedish) for news on the scene.

V

SNAPSHOTS

# ARCHITECTURE

Brutalism is the new black in Stockholm. In the past decade, the long-loathed socialist blocks of suburban Tensta, Årsta and Skärholmen – built in the 1960s and '70s as part of the Million Homes Program (Miljonprogram) – have found a new legion of fans. In 2002 architecture critic Mikael Askergren compared the concrete complexes to castles, predicting their future as heritage museums, restored to retro splendour. In 2006 Stockholms Stadsmuseum (p92) took the first step by transforming one apartment in suburban Tensta into a living museum for 10 days. Norrmalm's modernist icons Sergels Torg (pictured below, behind St Jakobs Kyrka) and Hötorgs-city featured in Moby's music video for the James Bond Theme in 1997 and fashion shoots can't get enough of the future-retro aesthetic.

Less controversial are the city's pre-modernist gems, including the Scandi-Renaissance Drottningholms Slott (boxed text, p40), baroque-rococo Kungliga Slottet (p38), national romantic–styled Stadshuset (p128), Nordic neo-classic Stadsbiblioteket (p57) and functionalist beauty Skogskyr-kogården (boxed text, p49). Of Stockholm's all too few cutting-edge postmodern creations, standout stars include stadium-cum-giant golf-ball Globen (off Map pp88–9, F6) and the Jetsons-like control tower at Arlanda Airport. For architectural enlightenment, don't miss a trip to the innovative Arkitekturmuseet (Museum of Architecture; p78).

| TOP FIVE ARCHITECTURAL ICONS | TOP FIVE STOCKHOLM INTERIORS |
|---|---|
| > Stadsbiblioteket (p57) | > Karl XI Gallery, Kungliga Slottet (p38) |
| > Skogskyrkogården (boxed text, p49) | > Golden Hall, Stadshuset (p128) |
| > Koppartälten (boxed text, p54) | > Biografen Skandia (p54) |
| > Stadshuset (p128) | > Lending Hall, Stadsbiblioteket (p57) |
| > Kulturhuset (p56) | > Kungliga Dramatiska Teatern (p123) |

# DESIGN

From Tom Hedquist Mellanmjölk milk cartons to Jonas Bohlin 'tutu' lamps, Sweden is a living gallery of Scandi style. This is the birthplace of democratic design dealer IKEA, and the capital's hotspots read like a who's who of Swedish design – Jonas Bohlin refitted Sturehof (p119), Thomas Sandell revamped Café Opera (p71) and Marge put the groove back into Moderna Museet (p12). Even the metro is a showcase of creativity (see boxed text, p58). While simplicity and functionality still define the Nordic aesthetic, new designers are challenging stereotypes with bold, witty work. A claw-legged 'Bird Table' by Broberg Ridderstråle and a table made of ping-pong balls by Don't Feed the Swedes are two of a plethora of playful creations from outfits like Folkform, DessertDesign and Defyra (p129). Industry darlings Front are an all-female quartet, famed for animated creations including a bin that bloats when full. Another trend is a revived interest in traditional Swedish handicrafts, with designers merging old-school embroidery and knitting with cutting-edge design. The source of much of this ingenuity is Stockholm's Konstfack University College of Arts, Crafts & Design, in the Telefonplan district; the area is set to become a major design hub with the proposed opening of a design centre in 2010. For now, the National Museum (p56), Svensk Form (p81), shops like Modernity (pictured below; p116) and Svenskt Tenn (p117), and the Stockholm Furniture Fair (p22) remain must-sees.

### TOP FIVE SWEDISH DESIGN ICONS
> Absolut Vodka bottle
> Carl Larsson's *Ett Hem* (A Home) paintings
> Josef Frank's floral patterns
> Solstickan matchbox cover
> Jonas Bohlin's 'Concrete' Chair

### TOP FIVE DESIGN SHOPS
> DesignTorget (p94)
> Konsthantverkana (p97)
> 10 Swedish Designers (p93)
> Modernity (p116)
> Svenskt Tenn (p117)

# MUSEUMS

Stockholm is mad on museums. The city's penchant for hoarding heritage has led to a hefty collection of 70 offerings. While few come close to rivalling the size or gravitas of London's V&A or Florence's Uffizi, many are sharply curated, interactive and fabulously eclectic, from the kooky vintage at Hallwylska Museet (p55) to the history of Swedish snaps at the Vin & Sprithistoriska Museet (p58).

Even cultural heavyweights like the National Museum (p56) and Nordiska Museet (p79) tend to think outside the box. In 2007 the latter hosted a design-savvy exhibition of Swedish wallpapers, while the acclaimed Arkitekturmuseet (p78) upped the ante with an exhibition of gingerbread houses. The Stockholms Stadsmuseum (p92) takes an equally refreshing approach to Stockholm culture, with past exhibitions spanning anything from the city's soundscapes to the history of food in the capital, while the Nobelmuseet (pictured below; p39) is more about ideas than artefacts.

Those with blue-blooded leanings have a number of palaces to peruse, including baroque-rococo Kungliga Slottet (p38) and Unesco-listed Drottningholms Slott (see boxed text, p40), home of the perfectly preserved Drottningholms Slottsteater.

But the talk right now involves Sweden's other royals, ABBA. The opening of a much-hyped ABBA museum, originally scheduled for June 2009 in the 100-year-old waterfront Stora Tullhuset, had been delayed indefinitely at the time of writing, due to complicated building renovations. Another long-overdue project in the pipeline is a major design museum, scheduled to open around 2010. For updates, contact the tourist board (p184). Not that you'll be twiddling your thumbs in the meantime, of course…unless it's Monday, when most museums take the day off.

# MUSIC

Despite local laments about too few venues, Stockholm's music scene hits the high notes. While Jazzclub Fasching (pictured below; p73) and the Stockholm Jazz Festival (p24) keep the city's jazz legacy kicking, the current 'it kid' is Swedish indie-pop, with names like Tobias Fröberg, The Knife and José Gonzáles stealing airtime internationally.

Unlike its Anglo counterpart, Swedish indie is less about attitude, more about melancholy. Good bets for a bitter-sweet taste include Fritz's Corner at Debaser (p105), Nalen (p74), Berns Salonger (p72), Pet Sounds Bar (p104) and Bara Vi (p103). Some of the best talent is signed onto the Labrador label (www.labrador.se), so check their website for upcoming gigs.

Equally booming of late is the dance-music scene, with thumping hotspots like Cocktail Club @ Grodan Grev Ture (p123), Solidaritet (p124), and electro-centric Marie Laveau (p106) luring the likes of French electro icons Vitalic and Alan Braxe and local heavyweights Eric Prydz, Sebastian Ingrosso, Axwell and Steve Angello, the so-called 'Swedish House Mafia'.

On the subject of clubbing, get set for queues and fussy doormen at Östermalm's 'it' clubs, where preference is often given to attractive, white, fashion-conscious females. For upcoming gigs, check venue websites or www.nojesguiden.se (in Swedish).

### TOP FIVE LIVE MUSIC VENUES
> Debaser (p105)
> Mosebacke Etablissement (p106)
> Jazzclub Fasching (p73)
> Nalen (p74)
> Södra Teatern (p107)

### TOP FIVE CLUBS
> Tranan (p75)
> Solidaritet (p124)
> Cocktail Club @ Grodan Grev Ture (p123)
> Marie Laveau (p106)
> Berns Salonger (p72)

SNAPSHOTS

# MULTICULTURALISM

With minarets on Södermalm and Turkish baristi in Norrmalm, Stockholm moves to a multi-ethnic beat. Decades of immigration have given this once white-bread metropolis a savvier global edge. Fusion grub is fashionable, galleries explore dual identities and local pop stars sport names like Salem Al Fakir.

Of Greater Stockholm's nearly 2 million denizens, about 80,000 are foreigners from more than 80 nationalities, with an even greater number of Stockholmers with Swedish citizenship claiming foreign extraction. The largest single group is the Finns (about 14,000), with substantial Middle Eastern and Chilean communities.

In neighbourhoods like Rinkeby and Tensta, migrants make up some 75% of the population. Often snubbed as hotbeds of unemployment and segregation, these so-called 'migrant suburbs' have become the latest in urban cool as out and proud 'blade' (a once pejorative term for 'migrant') embrace and explore the complexities of their identity. Suburban art hub Tensta Konsthall (see boxed text, p129) is one of Stockholm's hottest galleries, neighbourhood bash Hoodsfred (www.hoodsfred.se) pulls a 30,000-plus crowd, and streetwise suburban mag *Gringo* has become one of Sweden's coolest reads.

That said, immigration has become a contentious topic in Sweden in recent years. Claims of subtle but widespread discrimination, and a boost in support for the nationalist party Sweden Democrats, have challenged the Swedes' self-notion as a tolerant bunch.

Ironically, perhaps, while much of Europe tightens its asylum seeker intake, Sweden is opening its arms wider than ever. In 2006 the country recorded its highest ever intake of new arrivals – 95,750, of which 10,850 were Iraqi exiles.

# GAY & LESBIAN

Don't come to Stockholm expecting a Nordic Castro district. Gays and lesbians fit into the mainstream so well that there's little need to scream it from the rooftops. Same-sex couples get hitched and adopt, and there's even a 'homO' (homo ombudsman) for those rare cases of discrimination. Even at gay venues, crowds are often a mix of gay and lesbian, bent and straight.

For club listings and events, pick up a free copy of *QX* at bars, bookshops and record stores around town or click onto the website (www.qx.se), which also has a handy Gay Stockholm Map. All the rage right now are underground parties, sometimes advertised on *QX*. Your best chance of tapping into the scene is by asking the staff or crowd at glamfab Torget (p48). The bar is located in Gamla Stan, home to several gay haunts, including cute cafe Chokladkoppen & Kaffekoppen (p47) and the chic gayish bar at Leijontornet (p47).

Neighbouring island Riddarholmen is home to the hugely popular Saturday night Lino (p48), while battleship Lady Patricia (p106) is the perennial Sunday-night favourite, complete with drag acts, *schlager*-loving crowd and a packed-out seafood restaurant. Close by, rock club Debaser (p105) is home to the occasional gritty queer-alternative club night.

Left-leaning Södermalm is home to sultry nosh spot Roxy (p102), manly **Side Track** (www.sidetrack.nu), and hardcore fetish club **SLM** (www.slmstockholm.se), while up-and-coming Kungsholmen offers the laid-back camp of Göken (p134) and waterside bistro-bar Mälarpaviljongen (p135).

Topping it all off is the annual Pride Week (p24), Scandinavia's biggest.

SNAPSHOTS

# KIDS

Children are rarely an after-thought in Stockholm. From gardens to galleries, child-friendly spaces leave bubs in bliss and parents in peace. Museums often boast playrooms, restaurants stock highchairs and public transport is free for under-sevens. Best of all, many museums now offer free admission to visitors under the age of 18 or 19.

For family-friendly sightseeing, the island of Djurgården (p17) is hard to beat, crammed with parks, playgrounds and Stockholm's top kids' attractions, including storybook land Junibacken (p78), amusement park Gröna Lund Tivoli (p85), and open-air Skansen (p80), complete with animal petting zoo, dramatic glassblowing workshops and sugary Scandi treats.

The Swedes' knack for interactive museums means kids rarely get that glazed-over look, and the city's compact size means you can easily follow up a 4-D flick at Tekniska Museet (p113) with a spot of winter ice-skating at Kungsans isbana (p74). When you tire of the little tykes, simply drop them off at the Rum för Barn play pad at Kulturhuset (p56) and run off on your own. If this leaves you guilt-ridden, spoil the little gems rotten with super-cute Nordic outfits and toys from boutiques like Sprall (p117) and Kalikå (p43).

For up-to-date information on what's on for kids, check www.stockholmtown.se.

### TOP FIVE EVENTS FOR KIDS
> Stockholms Filmfestivalen Junior (p22)
> Stockholm Summer Games (p24)
> Stockholms Kulturfestival (p24)
> Luciadagen (boxed text, p25)
> Christmas Markets (p26)

### TOP FIVE KIDS' ATTRACTIONS
> Junibacken (p78)
> Skansen (p80)
> Gröna Lund Tivoli (p85)
> Tekniska Museet (p113)
> Spårvägsmuseet (p91)

# ECO STOCKHOLM

Boasting no less than 38 parks, Stockholm redefines the concept of 'concrete jungle'; an impressive two-thirds of the city's metropolitan sprawl is made up of greenbelts and waterways. Vegetable gardens grow in inner-city Södermalm (see boxed text, p105), locals swim at central city beaches and the Stockholm Marathon (p23) has been dubbed one of the world's most beautiful courses.

The capital's eco masterpiece is Ekoparken, the world's first legally protected urban national park. Stretching 14km from Ulriksdals Slottet (see boxed text, p123) in the north to Djurgården (p17) and Fjäderholmarna in the south, its network of cycling paths, walking tracks, and kayak and paddle-boat rentals make for a handy green retreat. The tourist board (p184) has information on cycling paths while www.stockholmtown.se lists a number of hiking routes in and around the Stockholm region.

Locals take pride in the fact that you can swim and fish for trout and salmon in the waters by the city centre; central Strömmen is the region's most biologically diverse waterway. To the city's east, the Stockholm archipelago (p20) contains significant populations of migratory birds, moose and countless opportunities for swimming, canoeing and trekking.

Those after a (literal) taste of eco Stockholm shouldn't miss organic garden cafe Rosendals Trädgård (p84) on Djurgården. In Gamla Stan, boutique Ekovaruhuset (p42) goes one further, stocking exclusively organic and fair-trade fashion and cosmetics for cool and conscientious consumers.

For further enlightenment on who's organic in town, contact **Ekologiska Lantbrukarna** (www.ekolantbruk.se). Other useful environmental sites include www.snf.se (in Swedish) and www.internat.environ.se.

**Opposite** Skansen (p80) **Above** Rowers at Djurgården (p17)

SNAPSHOTS

# SEASONS & THE CITY

Sharply defined by its very distinct seasons, Stockholm is a bit like four different cities rolled into a year. In the summer, the city defies Nordic stereotypes as temperatures hit the thirties and sun-kissed Swedes hit the shores of Långholmen, Djurgården and Kungsholmen to splash, tan and chow down on sublimely fresh seafood.

Long days and light nights set the scene for electric events like the Stockholms Kulturfestival (p24), midnight marathon Midnattsloppet (p25) and Midsummer's Eve (p24), when snaps-happy Swedes raise the phallic Maypole. The downside is that several city restaurants and shops close during July, when locals head to summer hotspots like the Stockholm archipelago (p20) for some seaside R&R.

Autumn brings blazing colour to the city's sprawling parks, with mild temperatures sometimes stretching well into October. Thoughts of a long winter ahead set the tone for spirit-lifting sessions at the Stockholm Beer & Whisky Festival (p25), happy homemaking at Hem (p25) and collective dreaming at the Stockholm International Film Festival (p25). Winter cranks up the cosy factor with its candlelit cafes, alfresco ice-skating and the Christmas market at Skansen, the perfect place for steamy *glögg* (mulled wine) and soft saffron buns. Equally unmissable in December is a traditional yuletide smörgåsbord, the best of which is at Grands Veranda (p67).

Indoor winter diversions include nail-biting ice-hockey matches at Globen (p22) and designer dawdling at the Stockholm Furniture Fair (p22).

Stockholm's spring is short, unpredictable and the time for Valborgsmässoafton (p22), when locals ditch the winter blues with bonfires and old-school song.

# >BACKGROUND

Flying the flag at Djurgården (p17)

# BACKGROUND

## HISTORY

### EARLY SETTLEMENT & MEDIEVAL STOCKHOLM

Rising land sealed Stockholm's destiny, as Swedish Viking political power was forced to move from northern Lake Mälaren to the lake's outlet for easier sea–lake trade. In around 1250, a town charter was granted and a trade treaty was signed with the Hanseatic port of Lübeck.

Stockholm's official founder, Birger Jarl, commissioned the Tre Kronor castle in 1252 and locks were built on either side of Stadsholmen using timber stocks, apparently inspiring the name Stockholm (tree-trunk islet).

After the Black Death of 1350 wiped out around a third of Sweden's population, Danish Queen Margareta Valdemarsdotter added insult to injury by besieging Stockholm from 1391 to 1395, amalgamating the crowns of Sweden, Norway and Denmark under the highly unpopular Union of Kalmar in 1397. The Danes' popularity wasn't helped by the Stockholm Bloodbath of 1520, in which Danish King Christian II tricked, trapped and beheaded 82 Swedish burghers, bishops and nobles on Stortorget in Gamla Stan for opposing his domination.

### THE RENAISSANCE

One of the 82 victims was the father of Gustav Eriksson Vasa, who managed to stir up a successful rebellion against Danish rule and become Sweden's first king on 6 June 1523, now Sweden's national day.

Vasa's sons, King Erik XIV, King Johan III and King Karl IX continued their father's nation building, transforming Stockholm into a major military hub during the Thirty Years' War and gaining Sweden an impressive property portfolio, including German and Norwegian territories.

By the end of the 16th century, Stockholm's population was 9000, and the city had spread onto Norrmalm and Södermalm. Officially proclaimed the capital of Sweden in 1634, the city boasted a thriving artistic and intellectual culture by 1650 and a grand new look courtesy of father-and-son architectural maestros the Tessins, creators of Drottningholms Slott (p40).

### RISING & FALLING FORTUNES

The following decades weren't as kind to the capital. Starving hordes descended on the city after the devastating famine of 1696–97 and the beloved Tre Kronor went up in flames in 1697. Russian military victories shrunk the Swedish empire, another plague engulfed the city in 1711, and King Karl XII was assassinated in Norway in 1718.

Feeling fragile, Stockholm swapped expansion for personal growth. During this time, botanist Carl von Linné (1707–78) developed the template for the classification of plants and animals, Anders Celsius (1701–44) came up with the centigrade temperature scale, and royal palace Kungliga Slottet (p38) rose from the ashes of the Tre Kronor.

While the reign of Francophile King Gustav III (1771–92) saw Swedish science, architecture and arts blossom, the theatre buff's tyrannical tendencies saw him assassinated by parliament member Jacob Johan Anckarström at a masked ball in the Opera House in 1792. The murder formed the basis of Giuseppe Verdi's opera, *A Masked Ball*.

## INDUSTRIALISATION & EXPANSION

When Sweden's northern and southern train lines were connected via Stockholm's Centralstationen and Riddarholmen in 1871, an industrial boom kicked in. The city's population reached 245,000 in 1890 (an increase of 77,000 in 10 years) and new districts like Östermalm expanded the city limits.

The elation of hosting the 1912 summer Olympics quickly dissipated when Sweden's refusal to uphold a blockade against Germany during WWI saw Britain attack the country's supply lines and cause starving Stockholmers to riot in Gustav Adolfs torg. Sweden's repeated official neutrality in WWII made it a hotspot for Jewish, Scandinavian and Baltic refugees, the first of many successive waves of migrants, most recently from the Middle East and Africa (see also Multiculturalism, p160). While the city's postwar economic boom saw the advent of Eastern Bloc–style suburban expansion, its shock value paled compared to the still-unresolved murder of Prime Minister Olof Palme on Sveavägen in 1986, and the stabbing death of foreign minister Anna Lindh at the NK department store in 2003.

# STOCKHOLM TODAY

While the worldwide collapse of the IT economy during the 1990s hit tech-dependent Stockholm particularly hard, the industry has since picked up, and the region is now also one of Europe's major biotechnology clusters. In its role as European Cultural Capital in 1998, Stockholm enjoyed a record number of visitors, while the city's renewed status as a progressive hub of design and fashion continues to pull in the savvy urban set. At the end of the noughties, cool-again Stockholm is feeling deservedly smug.

# GOVERNMENT & POLITICS

In September 2006, Swedish voters ended the 12-year rule of Prime Minister Göran Persson and the Social Democrats by narrowly voting in the centre-right Alliance for Sweden, a four-party coalition led by 41-year-old Fredrik Reinfeldt of the Moderate Party.

The traditionally conservative Moderates, who had only won 15% of the vote in 2002, bagged 26% of the vote in 2006, their best result since 1928. Behind the upswing was self-confessed 'clean-freak' Reinfeldt, who skilfully dubbed the party 'The New Moderates', realigning it closer to the political centre, focusing on the nagging issue of unemployment, calling for more tax cuts for lower- and middle-income earners, and (unlike his predecessors) tactfully promising to fix rather than ditch Sweden's welfare system.

But just how *new* the new Moderates really are has become an issue of contention. In 2007 the left-wing opposition accused the government of sliding back to the right after it announced the abolition of the property tax and wealth tax, both stalwarts of the Swedish welfare state. The govern-

## VIKINGS

Long before the first Expedit bookshelf, Scandinavians took Europe by storm during the Viking age. Between AD 800 and 1100, they travelled further than the earlier Roman explorers, settled in North America and Greenland, traded with eastern and southern Asia and fought for the Byzantine Empire.

Not all Vikings were warlike, though all were initially pagans, worshipping the likes of Odin, the one-eyed god of war. While cremation was popular, more elaborate are the impressive stone-ship graves, consisting of upright stones arranged in the plan of a Viking longship.

Rune stones were often erected as memorials and markers, and runic inscriptions were also carved on metal and bone. Sweden has around 3000 such inscriptions, containing a wealth of information about the Viking world.

Some of the most spectacular Viking art appears along with runic inscriptions, some featuring scenes from ancient sagas. For Viking insight, direct your sword towards Stockholm's Historiska Museet (p109).

ment has also proposed the sale of six state-run companies (including Vin och Sprit, maker of Absolut vodka), a reduction in salary costs for businesses, and permission for the National Defence Radio Establishment (FRA) to tap all telephone and internet communications in and out of Sweden in the 'Age of Terror'. The next elections will be held in September 2010.

# STOCKHOLM LIFE

Dishy dads pushing baby strollers are a common sight in Stockholm. Gender equality has advanced further in Sweden than in most countries, and stay-at-home fathers are out and proud. Parents enjoy 480 days of parental leave per child, children from 18 months to school age are guaranteed a childcare spot, and education, books and lunches in municipality-run schools are free.

Stockholmers are equally open-minded about food, with the average Stockholmer spending an average of Skr10,146 dining out in 2005, compared to the national average of Skr6196. Not that the good life comes cheap. Going out is an expensive proposition in Stockholm and locals tend to save up for the weekend and the days following the 25th of each month, the nation's much-loved payday.

Government statistics say the average Stockholmer earns Skr246,000 per year, is 39 years old and has 1.36 children. Although extremely proud of their city, many of the city's young cultural movers and shakers seem to wish it were more like New York – more bars and more buzz.

Of course, most will religiously defend the merits of their own neighbourhood and playfully diss their rivals – the traditional opposition between bohemian Södermalm and high-society Östermalm may be fading, but it's still kicking.

# ENVIRONMENT

Stockholm trialled a London-style congestion charge in the first half of 2006. Within months of its inception, the Swedish Road Association was triumphantly declaring a 20% decrease in traffic volume in the city and an increase in the sale of environmentally friendly cars, which currently account for around 20% of new car sales in Sweden. During the trial period, public-transport use increased by almost 10%, while greenhouse emissions in the inner city decreased by a healthy 40%. Hailed a success, the tax became permanent in July 2007.

**GREEN LANDINGS**

Scandinavian airline SAS is the world's first to implement green landings. Using new onboard technology, pilots can now calculate accurate landing times and exact runway specifications within minutes of takeoff, resulting in more efficient landings with less throttling up of the engines – a standard practice in conventional stage-by-stage aircraft landings. By reducing engine revolutions, SAS saves up to 200kg of fuel per landing, reduces carbon emissions by over 300kg and cuts down on noise pollution to boot. Initially introduced at Stockholm's Arlanda Airport, SAS plans to land cleaner and greener at all Swedish airports by 2010.

It's hardly surprising, really. Sweden is ranked as the world's second most environmentally friendly country in the Environmental Performance Index. Stockholm's industrial waste is strictly regulated, sewage disposal is advanced and efficient, recycling is popular, and strewn litter is as common as a loud obnoxious Swede.

In 2007 the city's Style at Sthlm fashion fair showcased a progressive collection of fair-trade eco-garments made by designers including Johanna Hofring and Lovisa Burfitt. The clothes featured recycled materials, chemical-free fabrics and fair-trade manufacturing.

Arguably less enlightened is Sweden's dependency on nuclear energy, the source of half of the nation's electricity. In 2006 four of Sweden's 10 reactors were shut down after the malfunction of two generators 200km north of Stockholm, sparking renewed political debate and mass fear of a Nordic Chernobyl.

# ART

Stockholm is home to much of Sweden's top-drawer art. Nineteenth-century highlights include the warm art nouveau oil paintings of Carl Larsson (1853–1919), the nudes and portraits of Anders Zorn (1860–1920), August Strindberg's surprisingly modern landscapes, Bruno Liljefors' (1860–1939) nature paintings and the vivid Stockholm landscapes of Eugène Jansson (1862–1915). Early-20th-century masters include sculptors Carl Eldh (1873–1954) and Carl Milles (1875–1955), whose work graces several Stockholm sites, including Tegnérlunden Park and Kungliga Dramatiska Teatern (p123). Milles' former home and studio, Millesgården (p19), is a city highlight.

More controversial was the advent of cubism. Initially met with caution in Sweden, artists who did embrace surrealist and abstract art include

Otto Carlsund (1897–1948) and Stellan Mörner (1896–1979), known for her bizarre 'dreamland' paintings.

Influences ranging from new realism to far left-wing politics heralded a new wave of subversive work in the 1960s from the likes of Öyvind Fahlström (1928–76), Lars Hillersberg (1937–2004) and Lena Svedberg (1946–72). Propelling this massive cultural shift was Stockholm's newly opened Moderna Museet (Museum of Modern Art; p12) and its visionary artistic director Pontus Hultén, who introduced conservative locals to American provocateurs like Robert Rauschenberg and Andy Warhol.

The mantra 'the personal is political' defined the scene of the 1970s, as did sharp critiques of the establishment, exemplified by Peter Tillberg's disturbing painting *Will You Be Profitable, My Little One?*.

While the 1980s and 1990s saw the rise of feminist-oriented painting, sculpture and photography from artists like Lotta Antonsson, Helene Billgren and Ingrid Orfali, interest in the relationship between art and daily life in the 1990s saw art move out of the gallery and into radical new spaces, as in the case of artist Elin Wikström, who in 1993 spent three weeks lying in a bed in a supermarket for her installation *Hur skulle det se ut om alla gjorde så?* (What would happen if everybody did this?).

Post 9/11, an increasingly international Swedish art scene has focused on globalisation, as well as the relationship between the individual and socio-political power structures, as seen in the films of Loulou Cherinet and the protest art of Fia-Stina Sandlund, famous for unfurling a banner reading 'Gubbslem' (Slimy old man) at the 2001 Miss Sweden pageant.

Often as subversive but more readily accessible is Stockholm's edgy underground or 'guerrilla' art, in which radical artists use graphics or graffiti to subvert or simply titillate across the urban landscape. Keep your eyes peeled for posters, flyers, logos and creative reworkings of billboards, check out www.akayism.org, www.krumbukta.blogspot.com and www.gatukonst.se (in Swedish) or grab a copy of Malcolm Jacobson's book *Dom Kallar Oss Klottrare* (They Call Us Vandals), an engrossing insight into Sweden's hardcore graffiti scene.

# FILM

The three big guns of classic Swedish cinema are Victor Sjöström (1879–1960), Ingmar Bergman (1918–2007) and Sven Nykvist (1922–2006). Sjöström, dubbed the father of Swedish cinema, started directing in 1912. Famous for personifying landscapes, his films include *Terje Vigen* (1917) and

*The Outlaw and His Wife* (1918). Along with Mauritz Stiller (1883–1928), who directed such masterpieces as *Körkarlen* (The Phantom Carriage; adapted from a novel by Selma Lagerlöf), Sjöström created a golden age of silent film in the 1920s. The glory days were put on hold, however, when most of the stars, including Sjöström and Greta Garbo, moved to Hollywood.

Acclaim for Swedish cinema returned with the work of the iconic Ingmar Bergman. While his arty psychological style initially disappointed conservative producers and critics, the international acclaim received by his film *Smiles of a Summer Night* (1955) had them reassessing. Bergman's partner in crime, cinematographer Sven Nykvist, is less well known; his skill working with light and shadow was absolutely vital to achieving the director's vision.

The growing power of TV in the 1960s caused cinema audiences to dwindle. Government intervention to save the industry resulted in increasing politicisation but failed to halt the decline. Only in the 1990s, with the rise of Scandinavian filmmaking in general, did the trend reverse itself, with young filmmakers like Lukas Moodysson injecting new verve into the form.

The biggest buzz in recent years has been the work of so-called 'second generation immigrant' directors, whose films have provided refreshingly new interpretations of contemporary Swedish identity. One of the finest is Lebanese-Swedish director Josef Fares' *Zozo* (2005), a tale about a young Arab orphan's struggle to adapt to Swedish life. Other highlights include Fares' Oscar-nominated *Jalla! Jalla!* (2000), Iranian-born Reza Bagher's *Wings of Glass* (2000) and another Iranian-born director Reza Parsa's *Before the Storm* (2000).

## TOP FIVE SWEDISH FILMS

> *The Seventh Seal* (1956) Ingmar Bergman – Max von Sydow plays chess with 'Death' in this chilling allegory.
> *I am Curious: Yellow* (1967) Vilgot Sjöman – Provocative political commentary was upstaged by frank sexuality for many viewers of this morality tale.
> *Fucking Åmål* (1998) Lukas Moodysson – This award-winning film (aka *Show Me Love*) is an all-girl high-school romance à la *Foxfire*.
> *Songs from the Second Floor* (2000) Roy Andersson – Hailed by critics, this is a surreal, grim but comic look at the idiocy of modern life.
> *New York Waiting* (2006) Joachim Hedén – Debuting at the 2006 Tribeca Film Festival, this melancholy tale of love lost is Hedén's first feature film.

# MUSIC

Swedes are the world's biggest buyers of recorded music per capita, and it's not all Alcazar and Ace of Base. Local tastes range from fusion, funk and dancehall to reggae, jazz and techno. The live-music scene tends to die down in one area only to revivify in another; while indie-pop is all the rage right now (see p159), nightly blues jams, salsa nights and classical concerts keep the scene diverse.

## CLASSICAL

Although Sweden has never produced a classical composer to match Norway's Edvard Grieg, there has been no shortage of contenders.

One of the earliest was Franz Berwald (1796–1868), who wrote chamber music, operas and four symphonies. Wilhelm Stenhamrar (1871–1927) was a competent composer of symphonic, vocal and chamber music, although his work has appealed more to musical experts than to laymen's lobes. Wagnerian Wilhelm Peterson-Berger's (1867–1942) opera *Arnljot* became the Swedish national opera, while *Svensk rapsodi nr 1, Midsommarvaka* of symphonist Hugo Alfvén (1872–1960) was influenced by a wedding he attended in the Stockholm archipelago.

Opera flourished after the opening of the Royal Opera House (1782), and since 1922 other venues have appeared, including the Drottningholms Slottsteater (p40) and the proletarian-friendly Folkoperan (p105).

## JAZZ

Between the 1930s and 1960s, Stockholm's jazz scene sizzled. While the late 1930s were defined by the Sonora Swing Swingers and their classic tunes (think *Lady Be Good*), it was Sweden's isolation during WWII that sparked a home-grown boom. This was the time of legendary soloists like trumpeter Rolf Ericson (1922–97), saxophonist Carl-Henrik Norin (1920–67) and clarinettist Putte Wickman (1924–2006).

Baritone sax Lars Gullin (1928–76) dominated the scene in the 1950s, with tenor saxophonist Bernt Rosengren (1937–96) grabbing the spotlight a decade later. Another star was pianist Jan Johansson (1931–68), who successfully fused jazz and folk in a peculiar Swedish fashion.

The rise of jazz-rock during the 1970s and 1980s, and a good selection of young vocalists in the 1990s and early 2000s, has ensured jazz remains a Stockholm staple. For a taste, swing into Jazzclub Fasching (p73) and Stampen (p49).

## POP & ROCK

After the Beatles visited Sweden in 1963, the Swedish pop scene exploded with scores of wannabes like the oddly named Ola & the Janglers and the space-age Spotniks.

By the 1970s a more distinctive Swedish pop tradition had emerged, led by jumpsuit collective ABBA. The fab four, whose career catapulted after winning the 1974 Eurovision Song Contest with 'Waterloo', enjoyed their greatest album success with their 1992 *Gold* compilation, released 10 years after the group had disbanded.

In the late 1970s anarchic punk groups such as Ebba Grön and Refused popped up to 'fight the system' while 1986 saw glam rockers Europe battle big hair with their international chart-topper 'The Final Countdown'.

While the extreme 'death metal' scene exploded in Sweden in the 1990s, the decade really belonged to MTV-friendly outfits like Roxette, Ace of Base, the Cardigans and garage band the Hives. Behind the scenes, Swedish music producer/songwriter Max Martin was to blame for the teen-pop revival of the 1990s, penning over 300 hit songs and producing albums for the likes of the Backstreet Boys, *NSYNC and Britney Spears. Spears' 2004 hit 'Toxic' was produced by Stockholm-based producers Bloodshy & Avant, who also produced two tracks on Madonna's *Confessions on a Dancefloor* album the following year. The same year, a string of Swedish dance hits, including Eric Prydz's 'Call on Me' and Stonebridge's 'Put 'Em High' cemented Sweden's rep as a house-music heavyweight (see also p159).

### FURTHER READING

Many of Sweden's most internationally acclaimed artists have been writers, chiefly the dramatist and author August Strindberg (1849–1912) and storybook queen Astrid Lindgren (1907–2002). Swedish must-reads include the following:

> *Röda Rummet* (1879) August Strindberg – Strindberg's breakthrough novel is a satire on Stockholm society based at Berns Salonger.

> *Kungsgatan* (1935) Karl Ivar Lo-Johansson – This novel by Sweden's champion of the proles created a sensation for its frank description of prostitution.

> *Kallocain* (1940) Karin Boye – A precursor to dystopian fiction like Orwell's *1984*, this classic depicts a totalitarian state in which drugs ensure the subservience of every citizen.

> *Ondskan* (Evil; 1981) Jan Guillou – A tough adolescent boy from Stockholm, beaten regularly by his stepfather, carves out a path for himself in an abusive boarding school.

> *The Great Enigma* (2006) Tomas Tranströmer – A sublime collection of works from one of Sweden's greatest poets.

# DIRECTORY
## TRANSPORT
### ARRIVAL & DEPARTURE

### AIR

Direct flights to Stockholm leave daily from several major international hubs, including New York, Chicago, London, Manchester, Paris, Amsterdam, Frankfurt, Milan and Bangkok. Most major carriers fly into Stockholm's main international airport, Arlanda, with a smaller number of mostly domestic carriers flying into the conveniently located Bromma Airport. Further out, Skavsta and Västerås airports handle charter and budget carriers, including Ryanair, and are connected to the city by buses.

### Arlanda Airport

Stockholm's largest airport, **Arlanda** ( ☎ 797 60 00; www.arlanda.com), is 45km north of the city centre. Terminals two and five are for international flights; three and four are domestic; there is no terminal one.

### Bus

**Flygbussarna** ( ☎ 600 10 00; www.flyg bussarna.se; adult/student Skr110/79) runs to Cityterminalen (Map pp52–3, E5), Stockholm's main bus terminal, every 10 to 15 minutes. The trip takes 40 minutes. Cityterminalen is located next to Centralstationen and T-Centralen Tunnelbana station. Buy tickets at the Flygbuss counter at Arlanda's main terminal.

### Taxi

The tariff to the city ranges from Skr445 to Skr500. The journey takes approximately 40 minutes.

### Train

The efficient **Arlanda Express** ( ☎ 020 22 22 24; www.arlandaexpress.com; adult/child/concession Skr240/free/120) will get you from the airport to

---

## CLIMATE CHANGE & TRAVEL

Travel – especially air travel – is a significant contributor to global climate change. At Lonely Planet, we believe that all who travel have a responsibility to limit their personal impact. As a result, we have teamed with Rough Guides and other concerned industry partners to support Climate Care, which allows people to offset the greenhouse gases they are responsible for with contributions to energy-saving projects and other climate-friendly initiatives in the developing world. Lonely Planet offsets all staff and author travel.

For more information, turn to the responsible travel pages on www.lonelyplanet .com. For details on offsetting your carbon emissions and a carbon calculator, go to www .climatecare.org.

Centralstationen (Map pp52–3, E6) in 20 minutes. Trains depart every 10 to 30 minutes Monday to Friday, and every 15 to 30 minutes Saturday and Sunday from 5.05am to 12.35am.

### Bromma Airport
Despite its handy location 8km west of the city centre, **Bromma** ( ☎ 797 68 00; www.brommaairport.se) services only a handful of mostly domestic airlines.

### Bus
**Flygbussarna** ( ☎ 600 10 00; www.flygbussarna.se; adult/concession Skr69/49) runs to Cityterminalen every 10 to 30 minutes. The journey takes 15 to 20 minutes.

### Taxi
The tariff to the city is about Skr300 with a travel time of approximately 15 to 20 minutes depending on traffic.

### Skavsta Airport
Situated 100km south of Stockholm, **Skavsta** ( ☎ 0155-28 04 00; www.skavsta-air.se) is popular with charter companies, especially Ryanair.

### Bus
Express services leave Skavsta about 30 minutes after each flight. The journey takes 80 minutes and terminates at Stockholm's Cityterminalen. Buses leave Stockholm

for the airport three hours before flight departure from the same location. Tickets cost Skr75 one way, Skr150 return and can be purchased online (www.flygbussarna.se), on Ryanair flights, at Skavsta airport or at the Flybussarna kiosk inside the Cityterminalen building (Map pp52–3, E5).

### Taxi
A taxi ride from Skavsta to Stockholm will take about the same time as the bus but will set you back Skr1300, making it a rather costly introduction to the city.

### Västerås Airport
Located 110km northwest of Stockholm, tiny **Västerås** ( ☎ 021-80 56 00; www.vasterasflygplats.se) services Ryanair flights from and to London Stansted and Dublin.

### Bus
Flygbussarna services leave the airport about 30 minutes after a scheduled flight lands, taking around 75 minutes to reach Cityterminalen (Map pp52–3, E5). In the other direction, the bus arrives at the airport two hours before a scheduled departure. Tickets cost Skr130 one way, Skr199 return, and can purchased online (www.flybussarna.se), on Ryanair flights, at the Flybuss counters at the airport or Cityterminalen building, or by credit card onboard the bus.

## Taxi

The tariff to central Stockholm is Skr1480, with a trip time of around 75 minutes.

## BUS

**Eurolines Scandinavia** ( ☎ 762 59 60; www.eurolinestravel.com; Klarabergsviadukten 72, Cityterminalen; Ⓜ T-Centralen) runs regular direct services from Cityterminalen (Map pp52–3, E5) to several European cities, including Oslo, Copenhagen and Hamburg.

## TRAIN

International routes arrive at and depart from Centralstationen (Map pp52–3, E6). Trains run daily between Stockholm and Oslo (six hours), and Stockholm and Copenhagen (five hours) via Malmö. See www.sj.se and www.swedenbooking.com for info and bookings.

## FERRY

Ferry connections between Stockholm and its Baltic neighbours are frequent and straightforward. Both **Silja Line** (Map pp52–3, G4; ☎ 22 21 40; www.silja.com; Kungsgatan 2) and **Viking Line** (Map pp52–3, E5; ☎ 452 40 00; www.vikingline.fi; Cityterminalen) operate daily services to and from Helsinki (15 to 17 hours one way). Viking Line also sails to and from Turku via Mariehamn (11 hours). **Tallink** ( ☎ 732 40 00; www.tallink.se in Swedish) runs several weekly services to and from Tallinn (15 hours) and Riga (17 hours).

## GETTING AROUND

Stockholm is a relatively compact city and best seen on foot. That said, the city boasts a quick, safe and efficient public transport system run by **Statens Lokaltrafic** (SL; www.sl.se). This book notes the nearest Tunnelbana (metro) station after the icon Ⓜ , the nearest bus route after the icon 🚌 , and the nearest tram route after 🚋 in each listing.

### TRAVEL PASSES

SL's 24-hour (Skr100), 72-hour (Skr200), seven-day (Skr260) and 30-day (Skr690) travel passes allow unlimited travel on the Tunnelbana (metro), suburban trains (*pendeltåg* and J-trains), city buses and the Slussen–Djurgården ferry service, including the Djurgården/Skeppsholmen ferry from Slussen. Purchase passes at Tunnelbana stations, Pressbyrån kiosks or main suburban stations.

The Stockholm Card (see p180) allows for unlimited travel, as well as free entry to more than 70 museums and attractions, and sightseeing by boat.

### TUNNELBANA & PENDELTÅG TRAINS

Stockholm's underground rail network (Tunnelbana) is the quickest, easiest way to get around town, except if you're heading to the islands of Djurgården and

Skeppsholmen, where buses and ferries are your main options. Each Tunnelbana line is marked by a colour (red, green or blue) and final destination, with all three lines intersecting at T-Centralen (Map pp52–3, F5). Services are frequent and generally operate from 5am to 1am Sunday to Thursday and 5am to 3am Friday and Saturday. Single-trip tickets (Skr20 to Skr80, depending on zones crossed) are available from SL centres, vending machines and train stations, and are valid for one hour from when the trip begins. They can also be purchased via SMS on the Telia and Tele2/Comviq mobile networks

by dialling 72150 and pressing 'H' (Skr30, full fare) or 'R' (Skr18, concession) followed by the letters of the zones you intend to travel in (eg A, B, C). Generally, the SL travel passes are the best value.

For travel information and train, bus and archipelago ferry time-tables, visit the main **SL information centre** (🕐 7am-6.30pm Mon-Fri, 10am-5pm Sat & Sun) inside T-Centralen, or call **SL** (☎ 600 10 00; www.sl.se). SL also runs commuter trains *(pendeltåg)* from the city centre to suburban and outlying areas. Most lines leave from Centralstationen (Map pp52–3, E6), with stations on the network marked by a J instead

## RECOMMENDED MODES OF TRANSPORT

|  | Gamla Stan | Sergels Torg | Stureplan | SoFo |
|---|---|---|---|---|
| Gamla Stan | - | on foot 15min | Tunnelbana/ bus 15min | Tunnelbana 5min |
| Sergels Torg | on foot 15 min | - | Tunnelbana/ on foot 5min | Tunnelbana 6min |
| Stureplan | Tunnelbana/ bus 15min | Tunnelbana/ on foot 5min | - | bus/Tunnelbana 15min |
| SoFo | Tunnelbana 5min | Tunnelbana 6min | bus/Tunnelbana 15min | - |
| Odenplan | Tunnelbana 10min | Tunnelbana 5min | bus 10min | Tunnelbana 10min |
| Skeppsholmen | ferry 5min | bus 10min | bus/on foot 25min | Tunnelbana/ bus 25min |
| Djurgarden | ferry 10min | bus 15min | bus 15min | Tunnelbana/ bus 25min |
| Fridhemsplan | Tunnelbana 10min | Tunnelbana 5min | Tunnelbana 15min | Tunnelbana 15min |

of the underground's T. One exception is the east-bound Salt-sjöbaden service, which terminates at Slussen, right below the Slussen Tunnelbana station on Södermalm.

## BUS

Stockholm's bus network is extensive and efficient. Most routes operate between 5am and midnight daily. After midnight, night buses operate a reduced service. The main night bus stations are Odenplan, Slussen, Gullmarsplan, Fridhems-plan and T-Centralen. Timetables and route information are available from **SL** ( ☎ 600 10 00; www.sl.se). Tickets can not be purchased on buses.

## FERRY

Djurgårdsfärjan city ferry services connect Gröna Lund on Djurgården with Slussen and Nybroplan as frequently as every 10 minutes in summer (less frequently in the low season); a single trip costs Skr30 for adults and Skr20 for seniors and ages seven to 19 (free with the SL Travel Passes).

## TRAM

From late March to mid-December, **vintage trams** (www.ss.se/djurgardslinjen) rattle from Norrmalmstorg to Waldemarsudde on Djurgården. SL travel cards are accepted onboard. Single trips cost Skr30 for adults

| Odenplan | Skeppsholmen | Djurgarden | Fridhemsplan |
|---|---|---|---|
| Tunnelbana 10min | ferry 5min | ferry 10min | Tunnelbana 10min |
| Tunnelbana 5min | bus 10min | bus 15min | Tunnelbana 5min |
| bus 10min | bus/on foot 25min | bus 15min | Tunnelbana 15min |
| Tunnelbana 10min | Tunnelbana/bus 25min | Tunnelbana/bus 25min | Tunnelbana 15min |
| - | Tunnelbana/bus 20 min | Tunnelbana/bus 20 min | Tunnelbana 15 min |
| Tunnelbana/bus 20 min | - | on foot 10 min | Tunnelbana/bus 20min |
| Tunnelbana/bus 20 min | on foot 10 min | - | on foot/Tunnelbana 20min |
| Tunnelbana 15 min | Tunnelbana/bus 20min | on foot/Tunnelbana 20min | - |

and Skr15 for seniors and ages seven to 19. Trams usually depart every 10 to 12 minutes.

## TAXI

Taxis are readily accessible and can be booked online or over the phone, or simply hailed on the street. The flag fall is Skr45, with charges calculated at around Skr8 per kilometre plus another Skr5 per minute. This rate increases in the evenings and on weekends. Avoid unscrupulous drivers operating unofficial taxi services from unmarked cars. Reliable companies include the following:

**Taxi 020** ( ☎ 85 04 00; www.taxi020.se)
**Taxi Kurir** ( ☎ 30 00 00; www.taxikurir.se)
**Taxi Stockholm** ( ☎ 15 00 00; www.taxi stockholm.se)

# PRACTICALITIES
## BUSINESS HOURS

Government offices open 9am to 5pm Monday to Friday. Banks are generally open 9.30am to 3pm; some city branches open 9am to 5pm or 6pm once a week. Most shops open 10am to 6pm or 7pm Monday to Friday, 10am to 4pm Saturday and noon to 4pm Sunday. Department stores and supermarkets often have extended trading hours; individual opening hours are given for each listing in this book. State-owned bottle shops (Systembolaget) open

normal hours from Monday to Friday, and until 3pm on Saturdays. Restaurants serving lunch open at 11am or 11.30am, while those solely serving dinner open at around 5pm. Closing time is usually midnight, although most restaurant kitchens close at around 10.30pm. Many restaurants are closed on Sunday and/or Monday. Bars and clubs are generally open to about 1am Monday to Wednesday, and to between 3am and 5am Thursday to Saturday; see specific entries for individual opening times. Museum opening times vary according to season, although major venues generally open 10am or 11am to 4pm or 5pm, with final entry generally 30 minutes before the closing time.

## DISCOUNTS

Many museums offer free admission to visitors under 18 and concession prices for students, seniors and the unemployed. Children under seven are also entitled to free travel on public transport. If you plan on visiting a lot of museums, it's worth buying a **Stockholm Card** (Stockholmskortet; adult 24/48/72hr Skr375/495/595, 7-17yr Skr180/210/230). Available online (www.stockholmtown.com) and at tourist offices, SL centres, Hotell-centralen, hotels and hostels, the card covers entry to 75 museums and attractions, sightseeing by boat (April to mid-December) and travel on public transport. To get maximum value, use two 24-hour cards over three days (with a rest day in between) and be sure to plan around individual opening hours, listed per attraction in the Neighbourhoods chapters.

## ELECTRICITY

Continental-style two-pin plugs are standard in Stockholm. Voltage is 220V AC, 50Hz. Appliances rated US 110V need a transformer to operate safely.

## EMERGENCIES

Emergency phone numbers:
**24hr Medical Hotline** ( ☎ 32 01 00)
**Ambulance**, **Fire Brigade**, **Police** ( ☎ 112)
**Apoteket CW Scheele** (Map pp52-3, E5; ☎ 454 81 30; Klarabergsgatan 64) A 24-hour pharmacy located close to T-Centralen.

## HOLIDAYS

**New Year's Day** (Nyårsdag) 1 January
**Epiphany** (Trettondedag) 6 January
**Good Friday to Easter Monday** (Easter Långfredag, Annandag påsk) March/April
**Labour Day** (Första Maj) 1 May
**Ascension Day** (Kristi Himmelsfärds dag) May/June
**Whit Monday** (Annandag Pingst) late May or early June
**Midsummer's Day** (Midsommardag) first Friday after 21 June
**All Saints' Day** (Alla Helgons dag) Saturday in late October/early November
**Christmas Eve** (Julafton) 24 December

**Christmas Day** (Juldag) 25 December
**Boxing Day** (Annandag Jul) 26 December
**New Year's Eve** (Nyårsafton) 31 December

## INTERNET

While internet cafes are common in Stockholm, the best value is the self-service **Sidewalk Express** (www.sidewalkexpress.com) internet stands, where internet access costs Skr19 per hour, paid by cash or SMS. If you don't use up all your time, save the ticket and log in again at any Sidewalk Express terminal. Locations include Cityterminalen and Kulturhuset in Norrmalm, Odengatan 47 in Vasastaden, Götgatan 91 in Södermalm and Arlanda airport. Most hotels have wireless LAN connections. Useful websites include the following:

**Allt om Stockholm** (www.alltomstockholm .se) Restaurant and bar reviews, in Swedish.
**Lonely Planet** (www.lonelyplanet.com) Information, links and resources.
**Temporary Stockholmer** (http://temporary stockholmer.blogspot.com) This sassy blog written by a local with a jaundiced eye toward his fellow Stockholmers contains good insider info for visitors.
**Stockholm Visitors Board** (www.stockholm town.com) A bit short on detail, Stockholm's official tourism website does have a useful events guide.
**Swedish Film Institute** (ww.sfi.se) Packed with facts about Swedish cinema and the local film industry.
**The Local** (www.thelocal.se) Swedish news, both mainstream and off-beat, in English.

## LANGUAGE
### BASICS

| | |
|---|---|
| Hello. | *Hej.* |
| Goodbye. | *Adjö/Hej då.* |
| How are you? | *Hur är det?* |
| I'm fine. | *Bra tack* |
| Excuse me. | *Ursäkta mig.* |
| Yes. | *Ja.* |
| No. | *Nej.* |
| Thank you. | *Tack.* |
| You're welcome. | *Varsågod.* |
| Do you speak English? | *Talar du engelska?* |
| I don't understand. | *Jag förstår inte.* |
| How much is it? | *Hur mycket kostar den?* |

### EATING & DRINKING

| | |
|---|---|
| That was delicious! | *Det var smaklig!* |
| I'm a vegetarian. | *Jag är vegetarian.* |
| Please bring the bill. | *Kan jag få notan tack.* |

Here are some common local dishes that you're likely to come across:

*blåbärssoppa* or *nyponsoppa* – blueberry or rosehip soup

*gravadlax* or *gravlax* – cured salmon

*Janssons frestelse* – a cream, potato, anchovy and onion dish

*knäckebröd* – crisp rye bread

*köttbullar och potatis* – meatballs and potatoes, usually served with lingonberry jam (or *lingonsylt*)

*pytt i panna* – equivalent to hash: a mix of diced sausage, beef or pork fried with onion and potato and served with sliced beetroot and an egg

*sill* – pickled herring

*smörgås* – sandwich, usually with greens, shrimp or salmon, boiled eggs, roe and mustard-dill sauce

*surströmming* – fermented herring; comes in cans which have a tendency to explode, and it stinks! Usually eaten outside for obvious reasons.

## MONEY

While not as notoriously prohibitive as it once was, Stockholm is not cheap. Count on spending around Skr400 to Skr800 per person, per day, on top of your hotel bill (much more if you're planning on A-list dining, clubbing and retail therapy). Seasoned budget travellers might get by on Skr300, excluding accommodation expenses. It's worth noting that many restaurants (including many top-notch establishments) offer half-price lunch menus, while hotels often dramatically reduce room rates on weekends. For currency exchange rates, see the inside front cover.

### ATMS

'Bankomat' ATMs are found adjacent to many banks and around busy public places such as shopping centres. All major credit cards are accepted, as well as Plus and Cirrus cards.

### CHANGING MONEY & TRAVELLERS CHEQUES

There are reliable exchange offices at major transport terminals, banks and post offices. **Forex** ( ☎ 0200 22 22 20; www.forex.se) offices offer competitive rates and low fees – Skr15 per travellers cheque, Skr25 for changing cash. No fee is charged when buying currency. Major international brands of travellers cheques can be exchanged at exchange offices, banks and post offices, although Forex exchange offices are generally (once again) your best option.

## CREDIT CARDS

Visa, MasterCard, American Express and Diners Club cards are widely accepted in hotels, shops and restaurants; supermarkets and many shops will ask to see ID. You're better off using the credit card, as you'll get a better exchange rate and avoid transaction fees.

## NEWSPAPERS

Stockholm's main daily newspapers are the thought-provoking *Dagens Nyheter*, slightly more right-leaning *Svenska Dagbladet*, and the more sensationalist *Aftonbladet* and *Expressen*. Both *Stockholm City* and *Metro* are free daily commuter newspapers. *På Stan* is the excellent Friday arts-and-culture supplement to DN. *Nöjesguiden* is a free monthly music and culture guide, while free newspaper *QX* covers the city's queer clubbing and culture scenes. Another good street press is *Odd at Large* (www.oddatlarge .se), with its focus on edgy fashion, art and culture. All are in Swedish, although the *QX* website (www .qx.se) has an English-language section.

## ORGANISED TOURS

### HOT-AIR BALLOON TOURS

Add some altitude to your sightseeing from May to September via these hot-air balloon tours (p16).
**Upp & Ner Balloons** ( ☎ 462 03 80; www .uppner.se in Swedish; Saltsjöbadsvägen 20, Nacka; flight per person Skr995-1695; May-Sep) Catch a Saltsjöbanan train from Slussen to Saltsjö-Duvnäs. The train trip takes 15 minutes.
**Far & Flyg** ( ☎ 645 77 00; www.faroch flyg.se; Gröndalsvägen 38nb, Gröndal; flight per person Skr1995; May-Sep; M Liljeholmen)
**Scandinavian Balloons** (Map p127, F3; ☎ 55 64 04 65; www.balloons-sweden.se; Kungsgatan 73; flight Skr1995; May-Sep; M Rådhuset)

### BOAT TOURS

One of the best ways to see this island metropolis is on deck, with numerous companies offering cruises through the waterways.
**RIB Sightseeing** (Map pp52-3, H6; ☎ 20 22 60; www.ribsightseeing.se; Museikajen 1; tickets Skr395; 1pm & 3pm Sat & Sun mid-May–early Jun, 1pm & 3pm daily Jun-early Jul & early Aug-early Sep, 1pm, 3pm, 5pm daily early Jul-early Aug; M Kungsträdgården) High-speed, high-thrill cruising through Stockholm and the archipelago on rigid, inflatable speedboats. Tours run for 90 minutes and depart by the National Museum. Call ahead.
**Stockholm Sightseeing** ( ☎ 58 71 40 20; www.stockholmsightseeing.com; M Kungsträdgården) Operates frequent cruises from early April to mid-December around the

central bridges and canals from Strömkajen (near the Grand Hôtel; Map pp52-3, G6) and Nybroplan (Map pp52-3, G5); tickets are available from departure points. Some of the one-hour tours are free for Stockholm Card holders, but the two-hour tour, Under the Bridges of Stockholm (tickets Skr190), is the most enlightening option. The 75-minute Winter Tour (mid-December to early April; tickets Skr180 to Skr240) takes in the city and archipelago islands of Fjäderholmarna on an ice-breaking boat.

## WALKING TOURS

**Authorised Guides of Stockholm** ( ☎ 50 82 85 08; www.guidestockholm.com; Skr60; 7.30pm Mon, Tue & Thu May-Aug, 1.30pm Sat & Sun Sep-Nov, Mar & Apr; M Gamla Stan) Informative, educational one-hour tours that are heavy on the city's 750 years of history. Tours leave from the obelisk at Slottsbacken (Map p37, E2) outside the Royal Palace.

**Stockholm Stories** ( ☎ 0708850528; www .stockholmstories.com; per person Skr200-300, min 4 people) In her guided walks, historian Maria Lindberg Howard tells interesting, quirky stories related to Stockholm's buildings, streets and squares. Call to book a time.

## TELEPHONE

Sweden uses the GSM 900/1800 cellular system, compatible with phones from the UK, Australia and most of Asia (and all tri-band phones), and dual-band GSM 1900/900 phones from North America. Almost all public telephones require a phonecard

(telefonkort), costing Skr50 and Skr120 (for 50 and 120 units respectively) and sold at Telia phone shops, Pressbyrån kiosks and newsagents. For international calls, it's better value to buy one of a range of long-distance phonecards from tobacconists.

## COUNTRY & CITY CODES

Sweden's country code is ☎ 46, and the Stockholm area code is ☎ 08. To call abroad from Sweden, dial ☎ 00 before the country code.

## USEFUL NUMBERS

**International directory inquiries** ( ☎ 11 81 19)

**Local directory assistance** ( ☎ 11 81 18)

## TIPPING

Service charges and tips are usually included in restaurant bills and taxi fares, but you will get no arguments if you want to reward good service with a 10% tip.

## TOURIST INFORMATION

The main branch of the **Stockholm Visitors Board** (Map pp52-3, G5; ☎ 50 82 85 08; www.stockholmtown.com; Hamngatan 27; 9am-7pm Mon-Fri, 9am-5pm Sat, 10am-4pm Sun; M T-Centralen) is located in the basement of Sverigehuset (Sweden House), opposite the NK department store. Apart from providing countless free brochures and information sheets (including the useful *What's On – Stockholm* booklet), the office can book hotel rooms and theatre and concert tickets, as well as boat trips to the archipelago. There's a souvenir shop and internet terminals where you can search the tourist office website. For information in English about the Stockholm archipelago, go to the Archipelago Foundation's homepage, www .skargardsstiftelsen.se.

## TRAVELLERS WITH DISABILITIES

Stockholm aims to be the world's most user-friendly city for people with disabilities by 2010. It's well on its way, with many museums, restaurants and shops suitably equipped. Transport services with adapted facilities are common; most buses 'kneel' at bus stops and Tunnelbana stations are wheel-chair accessible. Some restaurants may only have partial access and bathrooms may not accommodate wheelchairs or provide rails, so ask ahead when booking.

## INFORMATION & ORGANISATIONS

**De Handikappades Riksförbund** ( ☎ 685 80 00; www.dhr.se; Katrinebergsvägen 6; ☉ 9am-noon & 1-4pm Mon-Thu, 9am-3pm Fri & summer; Ⓜ Liljeholmen) provides information on disability-friendly venues in Stockholm. The UK-based **Royal Association for Disability & Rehabilitation** (RADAR; ☎ 020-72 50 32 22; www.radar.org.uk) can supply general advice for disabled travellers in Sweden, as can the US-based **Society for Accessible Travel and Hospitality** (SATH; ☎ 212-447 7284; www.sath.org). **Access-Able Travel Source** (www.access -able.com) is also a good resource for mobility-impaired travellers.

# >INDEX

*See also separate subindexes for See (p189), Shop (p189), Eat (p190), Drink (p191) and Play (p192).*

INDEX

## EAT

**000** map pages

**000** map pages